BACKCOUNTRY COOKING

The Ultimate Guide to Outdoor Cooking

SIERRA ADARE

Skyhorse Publishing

I dedicate this book to my husband, an amazing chef who created several of the recipes I included in this volume, and to our kids, who put up with me being very distracted over the holidays while I finished it. Thanks also to all those who trekked with me and field-tested the recipes. I owe a special thanks to my dear friend Chris Bendlin, to Anne O'Meara who introduced me to Jennifer Lawler who introduced me to my agent, Neil Salkind, and to my editors Ann and Kristin.
In loving memory of Clancy Adare.

Skyhorse Publishing books may be purchased in bulk at special discounts for sales promotion, corporate gifts, fund-raising, or educational purposes. Special editions can also be created to specifications. For details, contact the Special Sales Department, Skyhorse Publishing, 307 West 36th Street, 11th Floor, New York, NY 10018 or info@skyhorsepublishing.com.

Skyhorse® and Skyhorse Publishing® are registered trademarks of Skyhorse Publishing, Inc.®, a Delaware corporation.

www.skyhorsepublishing.com

10 9 8 7 6 5 4 3 2 1

Library of Congress Cataloging-in-Publication Data is available on file.
ISBN: 978-1-61608-312-0

Printed in China

CONTENTS

INTRODUCTION

TO COOKING BACKCOUNTRY STYLE

After a long day of slogging through mud up to your gaiters, the last thing you want to think about when you stagger into camp is "What am I going to fix for dinner?!" Nonetheless, after such a day, everybody, including the cook, deserves a hearty, tasty meal that's easy to make. Hence this cookbook.

Cooking Backcountry Style features a system for preparing quick, homemade meals in the field. The secret stems from whole meal planning and packaging before the trip ever begins. You can find all the ingredients you'll need at your local grocery store. And unlike expensive, dehydrated backcountry meals purchased from an outdoor store, the meals outlined in this cookbook cost no more than the average grocery bill to feed the same number of people for the same length of time.

If you plan to camp out on a regular basis, try shopping for your supplies and storage containers in bulk at warehouse outlets or online at camping and backpacking supply sites. Resupplying your containers from bulk supplies (flour, cornmeal, powdered milk, spices, beans, and such) will reduce your overall costs and maintain a ready resupply of ingredients for the next trip. Experimenting with dehydrating foods when they are in season will add to the variety and availability of your favorite foods when heading into the backcountry. Expanding your tastes with the inclusion of different types of seasonal food items will also increase your ability to provide proper nutritional needs while enjoying your trip.

HOW IT WORKS

In each of the sections, there are daily menus, a shopping list, and the preparations you need to do at home in advance of your trip, such as dehydrating foods for the meals. Then all you have to do is prep the foods for each day's menu and bag them by the meal. Although car camping meals require less at-home prep, it is still a good idea to gather foods and bag by meals the items that will not be purchased along the way. For trips needing dehydrated foods, begin the process about a month before the scheduled expedition to ensure plenty of time for dehydrating foods. Drying one meal's worth of ingredients together makes packaging meals easy and convenient. When you tackle the wilderness, a field preparation timetable guides you through what to do upon reaching the night's campsite, which dish to get on the stove first, and how to maximize fuel use by "double-decker cooking." The result—appetizing meals in a hurry. Tips on keeping foods hot, fast rehydration, and kitchen organization smoothen the flow from pack to plate, or bowl as the case may be. Usually within half an hour, starving, cranky backpackers, goat packers, horse packers, canoeists, or car campers become happy campers. Following every meal is my method for adapting the menu for each kind of trip.

A LOOK AT THE RECIPES

After you look over the recipes and realize they contain several ingredients you may not use at home, consider this: In the backcountry, your appetite will increase. How much depends on the exertion level, altitude, and weather conditions you face. People generally need one and one-half to two pounds of food every day in the wilderness. Winter campers require two to two and one-half pounds. If your crew eats with hearty appetites at home, you might want to do a test run. Try one or two of the menus at home (without dehydrating the ingredients first). Should every morsel disappear and the gang still wants more, increase the amounts in the recipes to accommodate. On the other hand, don't shortchange yourself by thinking you'll never be able to consume half a pound of trail food in an afternoon or finish off a dessert in the evenings. Remember, you'll be out there hauling around fifty to eighty pounds of gear, getting the most intense aerobic exercise possible climbing up and down hills or mountains, or paddling rivers. Horse packing provides a less strenuous workout (on you) than backpacking or goat packing, but guess who gets to lift those sixty-plus-pound panniers onto the sawbucks on top of a tall horse! Paddling all day burns calories, too. Car camping expends the least calories of the lot, and it is reflected in the smaller portions in this section. Therefore you might want to increase the amounts in these recipes should you want to substitute any of them for dishes or meals in the other sections.

While we're at it, you'll also notice salt sprinkled throughout the backcountry recipes. You may not use it at home (I don't); however, while backpacking and goat packing, in particular, your body needs more salt than normal. It helps your muscles work, and the harder you exert yourself, the more you lose salt through sweating. If your diet restricts the use of salt, feel free to omit it from the recipes. Nevertheless, check with your physician about carrying salt with you into the field just in case.

Margarine may not show up often on your table at home. I cook with butter or olive oil at home. Nonetheless, taking real butter into the field can be problematic as it can turn or melt and separate quickly, depending on the temperature. NOTE: If you usually use a nonstick cooking spray and don't mind hauling the extra weight, you can replace much of the margarine used in these recipes with the cooking spray. Unfortunately, at high altitudes where the temperature remains cold, the propellant can get a bit uncooperative. For winter camping in cold regions, I recommend taking margarine or butter. The fat content, in particular in butter, not only supplies energy you will need, it also takes longer to digest. This helps you feel satisfied at the end of the meal.

Coffee is not essential in the backcountry and might be another on that list of things you don't fix at home. Nevertheless, in the field, even nondrinkers love the way it can get your day started. Carry an extra bag of sugar and powdered milk or nondairy creamer for those who enjoy the supplemental goodies in their fresh brew.

Remember, keep food flexibility in mind. As the food coordinator, you should find out your crew's likes and dislikes, the amount of food and beverages they normally consume, if anybody is on a special diet or has food allergies, and plan accordingly. The key is variety and enjoyment, so substitute ingredients or have alternatives available in the field. Not everyone enjoys peanut butter, but it shows up in some of my recipes. Kids generally love it, and it provides great stick-with-you energy.

DEHYDRATING FOODS WITHOUT SPECIAL EQUIPMENT

With a bit of looking online, you can find great deals on inexpensive, yet durable, food dehydrators. Of course, you don't need any special equipment to dry the foods found in this cookbook. Over the years, I've utilized every method available to dehydrate every food imaginable. Sun drying tends to bleach out the color of food. Wood cookstoves work grand in cold winter months. A gas stove with a pilot light maintains a great, low-drying temperature. An electric oven or a gas range without a pilot light takes more fiddling. I've used all of these methods as well as a commercially produced food dehydrator.

The methods outlined in this cookbook work with all these types of dehydration methods. For making jerky, drying ground meat, rice, chopped onion, and any other small or drippy foods, line your oven racks with foil, shiny side down. Then on goes the food with airspace between each piece. Put the racks in the two slots farthermost from the heat source, usually the highest ones. Set the temperature on the lowest setting (or with just the pilot light if your stove has one). Prop the door open if food seems to be cooking rather than just drying out. (Watch the food more closely if you have an electric stove or a gas oven without pilot lights since their lowest setting tends to be a bit warm for dehydrating fruits and vegetables.) Check the food occasionally, turning it over often.

Depending on weather conditions (rainy or humid days retard the drying process), most foods will dry within twenty-four hours. Jerky, if sliced thin, should take no more than a day and a half. Unless drying meat, you can usually turn off the oven and shut the door overnight. Jerky is easiest to make if you put the meat in the oven just before bedtime. It's ready to turn over by the time you get up the next morning and generally dry by evening.

One of the best tips I've ever come across for successful jerky making is to partially freeze the meat first then slice it. This allows you to slice it nice and thin for uniform drying. Another involves the marinating process, which applies to meat or vegetables. Lay the thin slices in a nine-by-thirteen-inch glass pan, which allows plenty of room for the ingredients. Do not use a metal pan as it may give the contents a metallic taste. Spoon marinade sparingly over the food. Add another layer of meat or vegetables and cover with marinade until you use all the ingredients. Cover with plastic and refrigerate eighteen to twenty-four hours. Do not wipe marinade off before dehydrating unless directed by the recipe.

In the recipes calling for ham and sausage, I often use their turkey equivalent. Less fat, and I prefer the taste. However, feel free to use the pork version. The at-home and in-the-field preparation process remains the same for turkey or pork. Grind the ham or other meats by chopping it in a food processor. Or run it through a meat grinder, if you have one.

When drying fruits or vegetables, cover the oven racks with nylon netting (the coarse net, not the kind for bridal veils) purchased at a fabric store or any other store that carries fabrics. Then follow temperature settings mentioned above. There's no need to thaw any frozen vegetables before dehydrating. (It's usually less messy to place frozen food on the racks with airspace around them than if you let food thaw first.) Use fresh fruits for drying. With the exception of blueberries, frozen fruits turn mushy and won't dehydrate as well as fresh. Dip apple, peach, and banana slices

in lemon juice before drying. The ascorbic acid in lemon juice keeps these fruits from browning as they dry.

Since every oven behaves differently, experiment to see how yours works when dehydrating foods. Then note it in the cookbook for future reference. This may sound like a lot of work, but the first time you dish up Oysters in the Mountains or Lakeside Ham with Raisin Sauce at ten thousand feet, you'll experience the art and the ecstasy of outdoor cooking!

IN-THE-FIELD COOKING TECHNIQUES

Although hot water speeds the reconstituting process, waiting for water to boil consumes time and fuel. Therefore as soon as you reach camp, add enough cold water to the bagged items to cover them, unless otherwise directed in the recipe. By the time you get the kitchen set up and make a hot drink, the rehydrated ingredients should be about ready to cook. Or better still, get a head start on the rehydrating process by adding water to the evening's meal ingredients when you stop for a late-afternoon water or snack break. (This will mean carrying some extra weight for a short while until you stop for the night.) If foods aren't completely rehydrated by the time you set up camp and are ready to begin cooking, put them in a pot or skillet, adding water if it has all been absorbed. Cover the pot and bring to a boil. Pour in additional water as needed. Begin the cooking process once ingredients feel tender when poked with a spoon or knife.

The double-decker cooking method also quickens the rehydrating process. Place the bags of rehydrating foods on top of the lid of the pot of water you're boiling for hot drinks or while cooking the main entrée. A word of caution: Check occasionally to ensure the lid hasn't become hot enough to start melting the plastic bags. Also, keep the bags well away from the flames.

Always cover food cooking on the stove. In addition, create a wind block around the stove by surrounding it with packs or a piece of a closed-cell high-density foam pad (cushioned sleeping mats purchased at outdoor stores). Be sure nothing rests so close to the stove that it can catch fire or melt. These procedures reduce cooking time and fuel consumption.

Wasn't it Albert Einstein who said "time is relative?" That certainly applies to cooking in the backcountry. Since cooking time varies, depending on altitude and weather conditions, rely more on how the food looks and feels when poked with a spoon or knife to judge doneness. Maybe the recipe said the beans should have reached a mushy consistency twenty minutes ago. But they are still hard. Keep cooking them. If the edge of the brownies or cake has separated from the rim of the skillet and the center springs back when lightly touched, they are done even though the recipe calls for ten minutes more of baking time.

To bake successfully in the wilderness, you need a lid fire. Collect twigs between the size of matchsticks and pencils from a wide area. Pick up only deadfall. Do not use pieces from a live tree. While you're at it, gather some dead pine needles, leaves, or bark for tinder. Before you start your lid fire, select a cooking area sheltered from the wind if possible. Clear any loose debris from the site.

Once you prepare the bread, brownies, cobbler, or cake for baking, place it on the stove over a low heat. The pot or skillet should never be filled to the point the food will touch the lid during the baking process. Usually, you shouldn't fill the pan any higher than halfway before baking. Arrange the tinder on the lid. Loosely cover it with dry matchstick-sized twigs in a rough pyramid shape. Hold the flame of either a lighter or a match to the tinder until it catches fire. Add slightly larger twigs as the smaller ones start to burn well. After the fire gets going, distribute it evenly over the entire surface of the lid (for even baking). Replenish the twigs as needed. The flames should feel quite hot (but not to the point it burns) when you hold your hand about six inches above the fire.

Rotate the skillet or pot during the baking process to keep food from burning. Accomplish this by placing it slightly off center over the flame. Every few minutes, shift the position so another section becomes off center from the flame. An easy way to keep track of where you began the rotation is to place a rock on the ground at the starting point. For baking times of twenty minutes or less, five minutes per quarter (once around the rotation) is fine. When the recipe calls for longer cooking, divide the baking time by eight so the food goes through two full rotations. Allow baked items to cook at least half of the time specified in the recipe before checking on it. Otherwise, the stuff may crater and never rise again. (If the leavening agent such as baking powder gets disturbed in the early stage of cooking, it goes flat, kind of like an open can of soda pop left on the kitchen counter too long.)

When you do check on the food, let the fire burn to ashes, douse the lid with water, then gently brush the ashes (with a gloved hand) off the lid. Ensure no live coals land on the ground that could start a fire. After you inspect the food, resume baking by creating a new lid fire, repeating this process until the food is done.

Be sure to check with the Forest Service, Park Service, or Bureau of Land Management (BLM) to ensure a lid fire (or a campfire) is allowed in the areas you plan to travel through. If restrictions apply or twigs aren't available, the baked items in this cookbook can be cooked like pancakes, flipping them to cook both sides. Be sure to use no higher than a medium heat and lower it if your food starts to burn on the bottom while remaining doughy in the center.

NOTE: You can keep one pot of food warm while another cooks by wrapping a piece of foam pad around the container after you remove it from the stove. The Ensolite pad I sleep on is actually in two sections—one long and one short. The little piece serves a dual purpose.

Leftovers can remain in the pot or skillet and be reheated as part of breakfast or bagged with the trash to be carried out. Cleanup comes easiest when done immediately after the meal. Pour warm water into the dish and use either a pine cone, a clump of course grass stems, pine needles, sand, or even a snowball as a "scrub brush." If you use liquid soap (a degreasing soap works best), measure it out in drops; it is highly concentrated. It helps eliminate food residue and grease on dishes; however, if you don't get all of it rinsed off (and that's hard to do in camping conditions), it can lead to upset stomachs.

Discard cleanup water by pouring it through a sieve to catch any food particles. Empty the sieve into one of the plastic bags the meal was packed in. Perform all kitchen cleanup at least two hundred yards from a water source to avoid contaminating it.

THE CAMP KITCHEN IN BEAR COUNTRY

Again, check with the Forest Service, Park Service, or BLM to see if you should plan on bear camping in the areas you intend to travel through. It's a good practice some places in the Rockies, even though the locales haven't been designated as "bear country." (See the backpacking section.) On all trips other than backpacking, consider stowing foodstuffs, toothpaste, soap, bug repellent, and anything else that is scented in bear-resistant containers, built to withstand two hundred pounds per foot of energy without so much as cracking.

Otherwise, include a shovel and a thirty- to forty-foot rope, six to eight millimeters in diameter, in your equipment list. Select a campsite away from a wild food source such as a field of berries. Look for a relatively open area, preferably elevated (as on a knoll or hill). Set up the kitchen a good one hundred yards downwind, and preferably downhill, as cooler night air stays down in valleys, thus helping to keep cooking smells down low from your sleeping quarters and one hundred yards from where you plan to hang food bags. If there are no trees in the vicinity, double wrap foods in plastic bags to cut down on odors and pile duffel bags containing the food on the ground well away from cooking and sleeping localities. Two or three different piles some distance apart may salvage eatables should a bear raid occur.

Remove all items of food and things that carry an odor (toothpaste, soap, etc.) from packs containing clothing. The easiest and safest way to hang food bags is to tie one end of the rope around a rock and place the stone in a ditty bag (small stuff sack used for storing miscellaneous items). Tie the bag closed. Have everybody stand back. Throw the bag containing the rock over a tree limb twenty to thirty feet high. Tie the food duffels on the end of the rope and hoist them up until the bottom of the bags hang fifteen feet from the ground. The tops of the food bags should

also be dangling four feet below the limb from which they hang. Dig a one-foot-deep sump hole at least one hundred feet from the campsite. Dispose of all dishwash and rinse water, food scraps, toothpaste spit, and bodily waste in the hole. Cover the hole at night. If you use any canned foods, be sure to burn out the cans by holding them upside down over the stove flame to destroy any residue before crushing the cans and packing them with the rest of the carryout trash. Obtain more details from your regional Forest Service, Park Service, or BLM office. Or check bear camping information links from their websites.

A Final Thought

You don't have to go backpacking, goat packing, horse packing, canoeing, or car camping to savor these recipes! Skip the dehydrating section and fix them at home.

EQUIPMENT LIST

The Backcountry Kitchen (for every 4 people)

1 lightweight backpacking stove

extra fuel bottles**

small plastic funnel (for filling/pouring fuel into stove)

2 lighters

1 nonstick ten-inch skillet with lid (remove all plastic parts as they will melt if cooking over coals or a camp or lid fire)

1 3 quart pot with lid (remove all plastic parts as they will melt if cooking over coals or a camp or lid fire)*

1 2 quart pot with lid (remove all plastic parts as they will melt if cooking over coals or a camp or lid fire)*

1 plastic spatula

1 large wooden spoon

1 coffee sock (a cloth filter that resembles a wind sock on a wire handle) or a plastic one-cup cone filter holder and paper filters can be substituted if you don't mind the extra weight and trash to be carried out

1 metal or plastic fine sieve

at least 1 pocketknife

1 pot holder or cotton gloves

1 pair aluminum pliers

1 collapsible water jug***

1 flashlight with batteries (always install fresh batteries for each trip and carry/pack spares)

1 short-section foam pad (closed-cell high-density foam sleeping mats purchased at outdoor stores)

Backcountry Backups

camp matches in a plastic container

stove repair kit (to go with your stove brand, obtained from an outdoor store)

extra plastic bags

Eating Essentials (per person)

1 3 cup plastic bowl with tight-fitting lid

1 2 cup plastic bowl with tight-fitting lid (nests in other bowl, taking up less pack space)

1 12-ounce insulated mug with tight-fitting lid

1 spoon

Options for Goat Packing, Horse Packing, Float Trips, and Car Camping

cutting board, small paring knife, and chef's knife (to keep all these in one place, store them in a terry cloth sack made by sewing up three sides of a medium-sized terry cloth dish towel)

rolling pin

lantern (solar-powered ones are readily available from most camping supply stores)

small folding table

cast iron dutch oven and lid or second skillet with lid

double boiler saucepan set

a two-burner stove

plastic container designed to carry eggs in the field

vegetable steamer basket

can opener

grater

potato peeler

small wire whisk

bag charcoal bricks (variety that doesn't need lighter fluid)

small shovel

thermos for hot coffee or tea

pastry brush

paper towels

At-Home Preparation Needs

1 box of gallon-sized zippered plastic bags (freezer bags are best as they are heavy walled with sturdy zippers)

2 boxes of quart-sized zippered plastic bags

1 box vegetable zipper plastic bags (option for trips other than backpacking)

1 box heavy-duty aluminum foil

2 yards nylon netting (available at fabric stores)

food processor or meat grinder

food dehydrator (optional)

1 roll duct tape

7 small plastic bottles

1 plastic container with a screw-on lid (option for canoe trip)

1 box plastic wrap

*If you can find pots that will nest and create a double boiler, you can often use them to cook two dishes at the same time.

**When figuring fuel consumption, plan on using one-third to one-half of a quart bottle of fuel per stove per day during summer. (Check your stove's fuel consumption rates before going into the field.) Up this to one to one and one-third quart for winter. The higher the altitude, the longer food takes to cook. Thin, dry air allows moisture to evaporate rapidly, which in turn causes water to boil at a lower temperature. Cold and wind also contribute to depleting the fuel supply at a furious rate. (See "In the field cooking techniques" for a few tricks for on the trail.)

***Water resupply/filtration

Iodine tablets commonly used for water purification are still available; however, these days its easy and not very expensive to find efficient, lightweight, and safe water filtration units. Check with your local camping supply outlet or online.

Measurement Abbreviations:

T. = tablespoon

t. = teaspoon

pkg. = package

lb. = pound

c. = cup

pt. = pint

qt. = quart

Cooking Terms

Bake: Cook by means of a low flame on the stove and a lid fire. (See Lid Fire.)

Cut margarine into flour: Distribute margarine thoroughly into dry ingredients by literally cutting it in with the handles of two spoons or with two pocketknives, using a scissors motion, until the margarine becomes tiny beads coated completely with flour. (The dry ingredients will resemble rough cornmeal.) Butter may be substituted in equal measurements for margarine in any of the recipes.

Double decker cooking method: Rehydrating a bag of food on top of the lid of a pot containing food or water that is cooking on the stove.

Drizzle: Slowly pour a small amount of liquid or syrup over food.

Full boil: The entire surface of the water or liquid is bubbling in an agitated manner.

Lid fire: A small fire, using twigs no larger than a pencil, maintained on top of the skillet lid in order to create a top heat source for baking. (See "In the field cooking techniques.")

Low boil: Surface of the water or liquid just starting to become agitated.

Sauté: Using a small amount of margarine or butter to lightly fry meat or vegetables, stirring frequently.

Simmer: Below boiling stage. Small bubbles and steam may rise, but the surface remains calm.

Unless otherwise stated, all recipes serve three to four people.

Helpful Hints

Since many recipes call for small quantities of margarine or butter, it is more practical to add up the total amount to be used over the course of the entire trip and bag it altogether. Then in the field, measure out the portion needed for the individual recipe as all one pound or quarter sticks of margarine or butter are clearly marked for tablespoon measurements. A trick you can use to keep this process from becoming a mess is to grasp the bag of margarine or butter from beneath, unzip the top, fold the plastic back over your hand (like peeling a banana) and scoop off what you need. This also applies for nut butters or any other gooey items carried into the field.

Before leaving on the trip, insulate the three-cup eating bowls and lids by cutting and taping a section of Ensolite pad around them. Use duct tape for durability.

When mixing any type of dough or batter, start with a small amount of water. Reseal the plastic bag. Then squeeze it gently to moisten all ingredients. Add more water as needed in small amounts to obtain the right consistency. That way, you don't have to worry about carrying extra flour for dough or batter that has become too runny. If dough appears too crumbly, alternately add one tablespoon water and one tablespoon melted margarine until dough holds together.

Warm water works best when mixing dough or batter. It aids the rising of breads and cakes. Cold water can be used, but breads take longer and won't rise as well.

Accurately measuring water in the field starts at home. Measure water a quarter cup at a time into your two-cup bowl, marking the level with a permanent marker.

Potatoes dehydrate easier if peeled before slicing or grating.

If you can't find fresh green chilies, drain canned ones well. Pat them between a couple of paper towels then dehydrate.

Take molasses instead of a sugar-based syrup. It tastes richer and contains many necessary minerals.

When taking fresh fruits or vegetables on a car camping, float, or an animal-assisted trip, prevent spoilage by choosing under- or unripened pieces of fruit to be used later in the trip. By the time you need them, they will be ripe. Water used for cooking need not be purified with iodine tablets or purification filters prior to the cooking process. All the recipes require cooking times in excess of the five-minute boiling time suggested for purifying water. Water used for tea, coffee, or other beverages should be boiled for five minutes before making the drinks.

When adding fruit crystals to drinking water that has been treated with iodine tablets, allow twenty minutes for the iodine to do its job before adding fruit crystals.

It never hurts to carry an extra day's or two's worth of food on a trip, just to be on the safe side. Severe weather or an injury could delay you, and it's no fun to have to ration food or do without, especially if you are assisting an injured trip participant, both of you will require extra energy to make it out.

Unless you are hired to do the cooking on a trip, decide who will do which camp chores while the trip is still in the planning stage. A division of labor (one person cooks for the day, another fills water bottles for use in camp, another sets up the tent, etc.) makes camp life more comfortable.

CHAPTER ONE

HIKING "THE WINDS" FOR TEN DAYS

Recreational hiking is a twentieth-century phenomenon. Prior to 1900, people wandered through the wilderness for very different reasons. They searched for gold, fur, meat, or a better life; and they usually had a horse, mule, oxen, wagon, or handcart to carry their supplies. Nowadays, backpacking trips range from an overnight experience to an excursion that lasts weeks. The comfort zone, weightwise, maxes out around ten days' worth of provisions. If you plan to be in the backcountry for a more extended period, you should consider alternative means of obtaining fresh supplies.

One alternative is to pack provisions in critter and weather-resistant containers, then cache them along the route by either burying them or storing them in caves. Another option is to have somebody to meet you at a designated spot with rations that you have prepacked. Many outfitters provide such services, utilizing horses, goats, snowmobiles, skis, vehicles, parachute drops, or even backpacks to get additional food to you on the trail. Be sure to check with the Forest Service, Park Service, or BLM first. Many areas restrict the use of caches or the type of re-ration (e.g. no vehicle re-rations in wilderness areas).

Also inquire at the Forest Service, Park Service, or BLM office if any of the districts you plan to journey through are bear-use areas and require special camping techniques. (See *The Camp Kitchen in Bear Country* in the previous chapter for more details). Government agencies carry several brochures on traveling and camping safely in bear country or have links to information online. Also, in some areas, you may need special permits for using public lands. Always check with the appropriate agency before heading into these areas. In addition to have all the latest about campfire restrictions and safety information, they are a great place to leave a copy of your trip itinerary should you be delayed or injured, these are the agencies responsible for search and rescue. Although technology has changed, many of these backcountry areas still do not have cell service available.

With all this in mind, here are ten days' worth of backpacking menus and meals.

FOOD FOR THE TRAIL

The bulk bins at your local supermarket provide a cornucopia of perfect trail foods. In normal hiking conditions, figure on roughly half a pound of assorted trail foods per person per day. Include more salty type items such as cracker mix and corn nuts than sweets. For convenience, preslice the cheese to be consumed on the trail while fixing breakfast. Each group of hikers will have its own favorites. Mixed nuts, Sierra Madre Fruitcake, and M&M's chocolate candies generally disappear fast. I usually pick up the following assortment:

- corn nuts
- pretzels
- banana chips
- dried papaya pieces
- dried pineapple rings or chunks
- dried apricots
- dried apples
- pitted dates
- assorted fruit leathers
- peanut M&M's
- almond M&M's
- plain M&M's
- caramels (take individual wrappers off)
- licorice
- yogurt balls

- walnuts
- cashews
- sunflower seeds
- pumpkin seeds
- assorted hard cheeses
- Triscuits (or other wheat crackers)
- cracker mix
- assorted jerky (see index)
- Sierra Madre Fruitcake (see index)
- Summer Season Fruit Mix (see index)

SUPPLY LIST (10 FIELD DAYS)

Baking Staples

1 10 oz. can baking powder
1 16 oz. box baking soda
2 lb. brown sugar
1 lb. buckwheat flour
1 8 oz. container cocoa
1 lb. cornmeal
1 1 lb. box cornstarch
1 5 lb. sack white flour

1 5 lb. sack whole wheat
1 loaf whole wheat bread
1 lb. can powdered buttermilk
1 25.6 oz. box powdered milk
1 26 oz. box salt (I use sea salt)
1 1 lb. bag powdered sugar
1 5 lb. sack sugar

Crackers/Cereals

1 box graham crackers
1 box Grape-Nuts (or other cold cereal)
1 box Malt-O-Meal (or other hot cereal)

1 box oatmeal
1 box saltine crackers

Dried Fruit/Vegetables/Nuts (in addition to trail food)

3 2 oz. pkg. almond slivers
1 c. banana chips
2 lbs. walnuts
1 14 oz. bag coconut
1 8 oz. pkg. pitted dates
1/3 lb. apples

1/2 lb. apricots
1/2 lb. pineapple chunks
1 1 lb. box instant potatoes
1/3 lb. papaya cubes
1 8 oz. box pitted prunes
2 lb. raisins

Fresh Fruit

2 apples

1 qt. container blueberries

1 cantaloupe

1 honeydew melon

I lemon

6 peaches

4 pears

2 qt. strawberries

1 pt. raspberries

10 tomatoes

Fresh Vegetables

2 bell peppers

1 lb. broccoli flower heads

1 bunch carrots

1 bunch celery

3 eggplants

3 8 oz. pkg. mushrooms

11 onions

1 pimento pepper

4 potatoes

4 zucchini

Frozen Food

1 10 oz. pkg. corn

1 20 oz. bag green beans (or 1 lb. fresh)

1 16 oz. bag green peas

2 20 oz. bag mixed garden vegetables

1 10 oz. bag peas

1 20 oz. bag stir-fry vegetables

Meat/Milk/Margarine/Cheese

1 1/2 lbs. ground beef

2 lbs. beef roast

2 lbs. chicken breasts

2 lbs. turkey or chicken breast

2 lb. ground turkey

3 lbs. ham

3 10 oz. cans whole oysters in water

1 lb. cheddar cheese

1/2 lb. your favorite hard cheese

1 8 oz. can Parmesan cheese

1/2 lb. swiss cheese

3 1/4 lbs. margarine

Rice/Noodles

1 lb. brown rice

2 5 oz. containers chow mein noodles

1 12 oz. bag egg noodles

1 12 oz. bag vegetable noodles

1 lb. white rice

Sauces and Other Mixes/Drinks/Specialty Items

1 jar beef bouillon cubes

1 jar chicken bouillon cubes

1 lb. coffee (makes 50 regular strength cups)

1 can hazelnut-flavored coffee drink

1 jar orange drink mix

50 assorted bags of tea

assorted flavors of gelatin mix
   (including raspberry)

assorted flavors of fruit crystals

1 pt. brandy

1 6 oz. box corn bread stuffing mix

3 pkg. brown gravy mix

2 pkg. hollandaise sauce mix

1 pkg. turkey gravy mix

1 pkg. instant butterscotch pudding
   mix

1 pkg. tapioca

1 box instant cheesecake mix

1 12 oz. bag semisweet chocolate chips

1 bottle molasses

1 bottle soy sauce

Spices

1 container allspice

1 container anise seed

1 container basil

1 container black pepper

1 container cayenne pepper

1 container celery salt

1 container chili powder

1 container Chinese five-spice

1 container cinnamon

1 container cream of tartar

1 container dry mustard

1 container garlic powder

1 container ginger

1 container ground cardamom

1 container ground cloves

1 container ground coriander seed

1 container hickory smoke salt

1 container mace

1 container nutmeg

1 container onion powder

1 container orange peel

1 container parsley flakes

1 container thyme

1 4 oz. bottle Tabasco

1 12 oz. bottle Worcestershire sauce

Trail Mix

1/2 lb. per person per day (see list above)

21

DAY ONE MENU

Breakfast

Big Sandy Fry Bread with Spicy Sugar
Cheese
Coffee Sock Coffee

Trail Lunch

Jerky Pingora Style
Corn Nuts
Sierra Madre Fruitcake
Plain M&M's

Dinner

Lakeside Ham with Raisin Sauce over Rice
Mixed Garden Vegetables
First Night Cake
Tea

DAY ONE

The early July sunshine burns the chill out of the morning air as we stuff gear in our backpacks at the Big Sandy Opening in Wyoming's Wind River Range. Jeff, a veteran hiker, helps his dad, Dick, adjust the straps on his external frame pack. This will be the first time the two hike together in the Rockies. They ask me to coordinate the food and be the "official" cook on this trek to two destinations (in opposite directions), plus lots of picture taking in between.

In preparation, I confirm the food likes and dislikes and plan the meals accordingly. Since we all enjoy a few fireworks on our taste buds to start off the day, jalapeño cheese accompanies our trailhead breakfast. I also include a selection of gourmet-flavored coffees which the guys enjoy drinking at home.

Making camp coffee is like stepping back a century when it comes to brewing techniques. In the 1800s, cooks used a strainer called a "biggin" to hold the coffee grounds. Boiling water was poured over the grounds and left to slowly filter through into a cup. Then folks diluted the beverage with either boiling milk or cream. According to Mrs. Goodfellow's *Cookery As It Should Be* (1865), coffee prepared in this manner is "nutritious and agreeable."

Day One Breakfast Recipes

Big Sandy Fry Bread

1 1/2 c. whole wheat flour   **1** t. salt
1 1/2 c. white flour   **1/3** c. margarine
2 t. baking powder

At home, bag together all ingredients except margarine.

Spicy Sugar

1/2 c. brown sugar, firmly packed   **1** t. allspice
1 t. ground coriander seed   **1** t. ground cardamom

Mix and bag.

Cheese

Pick your favorite cheese for this breakfast or mix and match according to your backpacking group's taste preferences. You'll need about 1/2 lb.

Coffee Sock Coffee

1 T. ground coffee per cup of hot water

Bag coffee for the entire trip in a zipper bag. Use a tablespoon at a time.

In-the-field preparation

You can find quite a few currant bushes in the Wyoming backcountry, but they don't produce the right kind of currant for a coffeepot. So to make coffee using a sock, bring a covered pot of water to boil over high heat. Collect all the mugs. Spoon coffee into the sock. Hold it over a mug. Slowly pour boiling water through it until the mug is almost full. Add another tablespoon of coffee and repeat until everybody has a mugful.

Have sugar and powdered milk or nondairy creamer for those who like these supplements in their coffee. Once the coffee is made, pour enough cold water into the bag of fry bread mix to completely moisten the flour mixture. Reseal bag and gently squeeze it in your hands until well blended. Dough should be soft but not sticky. Melt enough margarine in the skillet to coat the bottom. Tear off a piece of dough and pat it between your palms until thin like a tortilla. Lay it in the skillet. Cover and cook over medium heat. Once the bottom side cooks and begins to brown and top bubbles up, flip it to cook the other side. Repeat until all dough is cooked. Makes 10–12. Sprinkle with Spicy Sugar and serve.

THIS MEAL *requires no adaptation in order to use on any of the other types of trips.*

The Big Sandy River cuts through a narrow valley accented with wildflowers. Chunks of granitic rock, mottled with lichen, squat beside the river. One piece, about the size of a backyard patio, provides a welcome perch for lunch. We unsling our packs, rub our aching shoulders, and climb onto the sun-basked surface. I fish around in the top pouch of my pack, extracting the afternoon's lunchables. Since we each chugged down a quart of water on the morning's hike, Dick and Jeff take our empty bottles to the river and fill them, adding an iodine tablet to each one to safeguard against water-borne parasites. However, it flavors the water like rusty pipes. After waiting twenty minutes for the iodine to do its job, we disguise the mineral taste by sprinkling some instant lemonade crystals in the bottle and shaking it well before taking a sip.

Pioneers on the Oregon Trail, which lies approximately fifty miles from our position as the raven flies, concocted their own version of "lemonade" to cover the poor taste of water. They mixed in a bit of sugar, vinegar, and lemon extract to pep it up. Our substitute lemonade quenches our thirst while we make inroads into the mixture of sweet and salty trail foods. By the time we lie back, satiated, to let the rock's warmth absorb into our achy backs, we've wolfed down the entire bag of fruitcake.

It, like the bulk of the foods on today's menu, weighs more than the foods scheduled for later in the journey. The heavy-to-light rule is something to keep in mind even on short trips.

Day One Trail Lunch Recipes

Jerky Pingora Style

1 lb. beef roast sliced thin
1/4 c. soy sauce
3 T. Worcestershire sauce
2 T. hickory smoke salt
1 t. garlic powder

1 t. salt
1 t. onion powder
1 t. ginger
1 t. Tabasco
1 t. chili powder

Partially freeze the roast. This makes it easier to cut into thinner strips, which in turn allows for faster and more uniform drying. Mix together remaining ingredients. Lay the strips of beef in a glass 9 x 13 inch pan. Avoid using a metal dish as it might give the meat a metallic taste. The larger surface area of this size pan allows you to distribute the marinade sauce more evenly. Spoon the marinade over the meat. Repeat with another layer. Cover with plastic wrap. Marinate 24 hours in the refrigerator. Spread the slices on a foil-lined oven rack and dehydrate. Or follow the directions accompanying a commercial dehydrator.

Sierra Madre Fruitcake

3 c. raisins
2 c. pitted prunes
1 c. dried apricots
1 c. coconut flakes
2 c. chopped walnuts

1 c. banana chips
1 c. dried pineapple chunks
1 c. dried apples
brandy

Grind the dried fruits and nuts in a food processor or put them through a meat grinder. Mix fruit in a bowl with enough brandy to hold the mixture together. Pack into 2 ungreased loaf pans. Do not cover. Do not refrigerate. Let sit overnight. Then slice the fruitcake and store it in plastic zipper bags.

By late afternoon we skirt around the edge of Big Sandy Lake. I drink the last of my lemonade and get a fresh supply of water from one of four creeks that flow into the lake, not adding fruit crystals this time. While Jeff and Dick look over the map, I remove tonight's dinner bag from my pack and pour some of my water into the ham and vegetable bags. Resealing them, I store our hydrating dinner in the top pouch.

We decide to camp above the back side of the lake. This means traversing a large marshy area. Ground gives way beneath each step as though it is like walking on a suspension bridge. Rivulets of icy water crisscross the open field. Pale yellow globeflowers and white marsh marigolds push through patches of unmelted snow, the result of the Fourth of July storm.

On a pine-covered knoll three hundred yards from the lake, we discover an ideal campsite—a split-level. On the upper bench a nice slab of rock nudges out of the soil to furnish a relatively flat surface for the stove. A couple of well-placed boulders assist in blocking the breeze. Trees nearby oblige as backrests while eating. Fifteen yards below lays a relatively flat open piece of pine needle–littered duff ground. Jeff digs the collapsible jug out of his pack and heads for the water. Dick gathers everybody's bedding, laying it out in the sleeping area. Meanwhile, I set up the kitchen.

After stacking the duffel bags containing extra clothing and gear in a semicircle around the stove to create a windshield, I unpack the food bags and check on the ham and vegetables. They have absorbed all the water I added earlier but aren't completely rehydrated. I add more liquid from my drinking bottle. By this time, Jeff returns. I fuel the stove and put on a pot of water on for tea. Boiling mountain creek or lake water for five minutes will kill parasites (allow a little longer at higher altitudes), so fresh, nontreated, water can be used for cooking and baking. While the water heats, the three of us scout around for dead pine needles and twigs for the lid fire for our First Night Cake.

Pioneers went to great lengths to ensure the fat or butter they cooked with didn't ruin. They packed bacon and ham in strong sacks, placed them in boxes, and stuffed bran around the meat. Since butter turned rancid quickly, they clarified it by melting it. When it boiled, cooks skimmed off the scum that rose to the top until only a clear oil remained. This was poured into a tin canister and soldered shut. Randolph Marcy wrote in *The Prairie Traveler* (1859) that butter thus preserved "is found to keep sweet for a great length of time, and its flavor is but little impaired by the process."

Day One Dinner Recipes

Lakeside Ham with Raisin Sauce

12 slices ham, ground	**1** t. allspice
1 c. raisins	**1** t. mace
2 c. brown sugar, firmly packed	**1** t. ground cloves
2 t. cinnamon	**2** t. powdered mustard

Cut fully cooked ham slices in your normal serving portions then grind them in a food processor or meat grinder. Dehydrate ham and bag. Mix remaining ingredients and bag.

Rice

1 1/2 c. white rice   **1 1/2** c. water

In a covered pot, bring rice and water to a boil. Add 1/3 c. more cold water. Simmer, covered, 20 to 25 minutes. When cooked, spread on foil-covered oven racks and dry. Or dry according to your dehydrator's directions.

Mixed Garden Vegetables

1 1/3 20-oz. bags of frozen mixed garden vegetables Spread on foil-covered oven racks and dry. No need to thaw first.

First Night Cake

1 c. flour   **1** t. baking powder
1/2 c. brown sugar, firmly packed   **1** t. baking soda
1/2 t. allspice   **1** t. salt
1/2 t. nutmeg   **1/2** c. raisins
1/2 t. ginger   **1/2** c. oatmeal
1 t. anise seed   **1/2** c. plus 2 T. margarine

Mix together and bag all ingredients except margarine.

In-the-field preparation

As soon as you reach the night's camping spot, pour enough cold water into the bags of ham and mixed vegetables to cover the ingredients and reseal (if you haven't started the hydration process on the trail). Do not add cold water to the rice, sauce, or cake mix. Meanwhile, put a large covered pot of water on the stove for hot tea. Bring to a boil over high heat while you collect everybody's mug and big insulated bowl and lid. Then gather dry dead leaves or pine needles and small twigs for the lid fire. Locate your lighter. Divide rice between the four bowls. When water boils, pour 1/3 c. of the boiling water over each bowl of rice. Put the lids on and set aside. The rice needs at least 8–10 minutes to reconstitute.

Once you've made a mug of tea for everybody, pour the soaking ham into the pot and set aside. Pour the mixed vegetables into the saucepan. Cover and bring to a boil over high heat. As soon as they are at a full boil, remove from the stove. Put the ham over the flame. Add sauce mix and 2 c. cold water. Cover and bring to a boil. Employ the double-decker method to keep the vegetables hot while the ham cooks. When it starts to boil, reduce to low heat and simmer until meat and vegetables are tender (approximately 20 minutes, depending on altitude). Stir ham frequently. Add more water if sauce becomes too thick. It should have the consistency of syrup. If vegetables aren't completely tender when ham is cooked, bring them to boil while you serve the ham over the rice.

During dinner, melt 1/2 c. margarine in a large pot over medium heat (no need to clean it out after cooking ham). Remove from heat. Add cake mix and 2 T. cold water.

Blend until dry ingredients are moistened, adding a splash more water if necessary to form a stiff dough. Melt remaining margarine in the skillet, swirling to coat bottom and sides. Pat dough into skillet. Bake over low heat and a lid fire 40–45 minutes, rotating pan to keep the cake from burning. When cake is done, put a covered pot of water on to boil for another round of tea and for washup.

__AS AN OPTION__ on goat, horse, float, or car camping trips, pack frozen ham steaks instead of drying them. Canned mixed vegetables can also replace dehydrated ones. NOTE: on goat trips, carrying the heavier fresh, frozen, or canned foods will mean bringing an additional goat to accommodate the extra weight.

We can't finish off the cake, so I put the leftovers in a clean plastic bag and put it in my pack to have handy for trail food tomorrow. After a last round of tea, Dick collects the dishes. Any scraps of food get scraped into one of the empty plastic bags from dinner. Next he swirls hot water in each container, using a clump of pine needles to scrub out the dishes. Jeff holds the sieve, and Dick strain the wash water through it to catch any food particles loosened by the scrub brush. He dumps the contents of the sieve into the scrap bag. Then they rinse the dishes in hot water and store them in a duffel. A quick check of tomorrow's breakfast menu shows nothing that needs to be soaked overnight.

DAY TWO MENU

Breakfast

Mountain Gruel

Coffee

Trail Lunch

Cheese

Triscuits

Dried Apples

Peanut M&M's

Dinner

Switchback

Bridger Buttermilk Brownies

Tea

DAY TWO

People used to refer to cereals by the unflattering name of "gruel." Cooks prepared it by boiling water in a skillet and throwing in handfuls of oats or other grains and sometimes adding raisins. After the concoction boiled for ten minutes, they poured it in bowls, added salt, sugar, and nutmeg.

Day Two Breakfast Recipe

Mountain Gruel

2/3 c. papaya cubes   **3/4** c. sugar
2/3 c. nuts   **3** T. powdered milk
1 1/3 c. Malt-O-Meal   **1/2** t. nutmeg

Bag papaya separately from remaining ingredients.

In-the-field preparation

After the coffee water boils, pour 1 1/3 c. of cold water and the papaya in a pot. Cover. Bring to boil over low heat. Stir in Malt-O-Meal mix. Cook 1 minute. Serve with extra powdered milk if desired.

THIS MEAL *requires no adaptation for the other kinds of trips.*

Once we finish breakfast and do the dishes, we make a final sweep of the site, checking for any food scraps or items we might have overlooked during packing. We erase all evidence of the camp by scattering the pine needles, pebbles, and duff soil dislodged last night in the sleeping area.

Next we hoist our packs onto our backs and recross the marsh to the base of Jackass Pass. There's a good reason this path is so named. As one story goes, in olden days, the steep rugged route defied all means of transport except for the sure-footed jackasses. Hikers, however, tell a different tale as the pass gains one thousand feet in elevation in little over a mile. Switchbacks zigzag up a sheer mountainside from the trailhead. Panting, we pause for breath several times, our boots punch through ice-crusted snow on the trail. Patches of it intermingle with one boulder field after another—the rubble left by glaciation and erosion. We scramble over them, certain our lungs will burst. But nature soon gives us a break, allowing us to head down a narrow corridor to the shore of North Lake. Sundance Pinnacle surges up out of the left corner of the dark blue water. Sheltered in a nook between boulders scattered near the lake, we lunch on a variety of cheeses and crackers, M&M's, leftover cake, and dried apple slices.

More often than not, eighteenth- and nineteenth-century shoppers could obtain dried apples far more readily than fresh. After the Civil War, the wife of an army officer stationed in the Dakota Territory paid the outrageous sum of twenty-five dollars to have a barrel of apples shipped to her from Oregon. Regardless of price, when an abundance of fresh could be obtained, the apples were peeled, cut into quarters, strung like beads on a necklace, and hung near the fireplace or kitchen stove to dry. Oven drying is a whole lot easier!

Before hitting the trail again, we fill our water bottles from the confluence of North Creek and the lake. I also pour some water over the turkey-and-eggplant mixture for dinner. Taking a hearty breath, the three of us traverse the rocky beach and continue the trek. Another set of switchbacks leads up a rock-littered incline dotted with pines. Intermittent streams of sun-melted snow crisscross the path. A sheltered cavity recessed in the trees presents an adequate camping spot. Once unpacked, I start water for tea, placing the bag of rehydrating meat and vegetables on the lid to speed up the process. I keep an eye on the bag while I collect mugs and bowls to ensure it doesn't shift and get too near the flame or that the lid becomes hot enough to melt the plastic.

Day Two Dinner Recipes

Switchback

1 lb. ground turkey
1 1/2 eggplant, chopped
4 tomatoes
1 bell pepper, chopped

1 onion
1/2 c. Parmesan cheese
3 c. egg noodles

Brown turkey then dehydrate with eggplant, tomatoes, pepper, and onion. Bag together. Put noodles and cheese into separate bags.

Bridger Buttermilk Brownies

1/4 c. cocoa
1 c. flour
1 T. hazelnut flavored coffee drink
3/4 c. sugar

1 t. baking powder
1 t. salt
2 T. powdered buttermilk
1/2 c. margarine

Mix dry ingredients. Bag together except for margarine.

In-the-field preparation

Upon your arrival in camp (if you haven't started the process on a trail break), pour enough cold water into the bag of dry turkey and vegetables to cover and reseal. Do not add water to the noodles. Once everybody has a hot drink, pour the soaking turkey mixture into the pot. Cover and bring to a boil over high heat.

Reduce to medium heat and cook until meat and vegetables are tender, 20-30 minutes. Stir frequently. Add more water as needed to keep meat and vegetables covered. When turkey mixture is cooked, add enough water to cover ingredients again (if necessary) and bring back to boil over high heat. Add noodles. Cook over medium heat until noodles are done, about 10 minutes more. Stir frequently. When done, remove from heat and add cheese.

During dinner, melt 1/2 c. margarine in the skillet. Add 1 c. cold water then pour this into the bag of brownie mix. Reseal. Squeeze gently until completely moistened. It should be a thick batter. Pour batter into the skillet. Bake over low heat with a lid fire for 45–50 minutes, rotating for even cooking.

After cleanup, you can get a head start on the rehydration process for tomorrow. Check the breakfast menu and add cold water to the meat and vegetables tonight before going to bed.

AS AN OPTION *on car camping, goat, or horse trips, substitute a tube of frozen ground turkey, fresh eggplant, and bell pepper, and 1 28 oz. can of whole tomatoes, provided this meal is prepared no later than the second day as the meat will spoil. On float trips, pack frozen turkey and fresh vegetables in an ice chest, but fix no later than three days into the journey.*

DAY THREE MENU

Breakfast

Packer's Ham Hashbrowns

Coffee

Trail Lunch

Dried Apricots

Pretzels

Sunflower Seeds

Cashews

Yogurt Balls

Dinner

Oysters in the Mountains

Triple Sock Tapioca

Tea

DAY THREE

In the nineteenth century, people rarely ate fresh pork roast. They either smoke cured or stored it in a salt brine (salt pork) or they made ham. To do this, pilgrims soaked pork roasts a couple of weeks in a mixture of saltwater, sugar or molasses, and spices. Once removed from this solution, the meat hung in a smokehouse for several weeks, absorbing a thick cloud of oak, hickory, or maple smoke. Then the meat was rubbed with pepper, put in a muslin bag, and hung in a root cellar. When cooks prepared ham, they scrapped off any mold that accumulated on the rind with a knife. Next they vigorously scrubbed the ham with soap suds and a brush, rinsed the meat in hot water and soaked it thirty-six hours (or longer for older hams) before baking it eighteen minutes for every pound of meat. Thanks to a bit of prior planning last night, I fix our Packer's Ham Hashbrowns in next to no time.

Day Three Breakfast Recipes

Packer's Ham Hashbrowns

4 slices of ham, ground
4 potatoes, grated
2 tomatoes, chopped
1/2 t. salt

1 t. pepper
1/4 lb. cheddar cheese
2 T. margarine

Dehydrate ham, potatoes, and tomatoes. Bag ham and potatoes together. Combine salt and pepper with the tomatoes. Bag cheese separately.

In-the-field preparation

Rehydrate ham and vegetables while you make morning hot drinks (if you didn't start the process last night). Melt margarine in the skillet. Add ham and potatoes. Cover and fry over medium heat, flipping once as hash browns brown. Lay cheese on top. Cover. Reduce heat to low and cook until cheese melts. Serve with tomato on top.

__AS AN OPTION__ on goat and horse trips, substitute canned ham and fresh potatoes. For float expeditions and car camping, substitute ham steaks that have been frozen and a 20 oz. bag of frozen hash browns, and fresh tomatoes. Store in an ice chest and fix no later than the third morning.

Bear tracks, no more than a few hours old, punctuate the snowy edge of frozen Arrowhead Lake high along Jackass Pass. The animal had crossed the lake and wandered up and over the pass. Our tracks parallel the bear's along the thin strip of shore. This isn't Jeff's, and by no means closest, encounter with members of the Ursid family in areas they supposedly don't inhabit. By unanimous decision, we vote to rig for bear camping when we set up tonight's bivouac.

On top of Jackass Pass, elevation 10,800 feet, we straddle the Continental Divide on a rock-strewn, wind-scoured tundra. Seven hundred feet in the basin below, Lonesome Lake acts like a miniature reflecting pool for the surrounding peaks of the Cirque of the Towers, a collection of sheer rock faces, scarred and hollowed into a foreboding semicircle by glaciers during the Pleistocene Era. The ridge we walk offers slender benches of land and stone that allow an escape from the relentless gale that steals our breath the instant we expel it. We drop down into the little bowl-shaped valley. Pine trees radiate out from the perimeter of the lake well away from any bear tracks in the snow and soil, offering excellent possibilities for bear camping.

First we designate the kitchen, sleeping area, and a good location to hang the food bags. Jeff rigs the rope. Dick digs the sump hole, and I set up the kitchen. I remove tonight's dinner and dessert bags and add water to the oysters and peas. While I prepare the meal, the guys double wrap all food items in plastic bags and have bags ready to store dishes, toothpaste, and soap in after we finish a last mug of tea and our tapioca pudding.

Back in the early 1800s, cooks reserved the term "pudding" for desserts with a flour or cornmeal base. They classified tapioca as a "jelly." It had to be soaked for five or six hours then simmered in the same water and bits of fresh lemon peel until the liquid became quite clear, usually a couple of hours or more. A little wine, lemon juice, and sugar were then mixed with the tapioca before serving.

Day Three Dinner Recipes

Oysters in the Mountain

3 10 oz. cans whole oysters in water
1 16 oz. bag frozen green peas

4 chicken bouillon cubes
4 T. margarine

Dumpling Mix

3 c. whole wheat flour

2 t. salt

2 t. baking powder

2 t. baking soda

6 T. powdered milk

2 T. parsley flakes

2 t. pepper

1 t. mace

1 t. nutmeg

Dehydrate oysters and peas. Do not thaw peas before drying. Combine Dumpling Mix ingredients in a zipper plastic bag. Take the wrappers off of the bouillon cubes and bag with the dried oysters. Store peas and margarine by themselves.

Triple Sock Tapioca

1/3 c. sugar

2 T. brown sugar, firmly packed

3 T. cocoa

1/2 c. raisins

4 T. tapioca

1 t. cinnamon

1/2 c. powdered milk

1/4 c. margarine

Bag all ingredients together, except margarine.

In-the-field preparation

Reconstitute the oysters by filling the bag 3/4 of the way full with water. Reseal and set aside. Soak peas in just enough cold water to cover them. While water heats for hot drinks, cut 4 T. margarine into the dumpling mix. Add 1 1/3 to 1 1/2 c. cold water to make a stiff dough. Pour the excess oyster reconstituting liquid in the large pot, adding enough cold water to bring the liquid level to half full. Cover and bring to a boil over high heat. Form balls of dumpling mix around individual oysters. Drop dumplings in the boiling water. There should be approximately a third of the oysters left after the dough runs out. Add remaining oysters to dumplings and water. Adjust heat to maintain a low boil, cooking 15–20 minutes. Melt 1/4 c. margarine in the smaller pot. Add 3 c. cold water and dry tapioca ingredients. Soak 5 minutes. Cover. Bring to boil over medium heat. Stir often. This is very rich!

__AS AN OPTION__ for car camping, goat, horse, and float trips, substitute canned oysters and peas. The remaining recipes need no adaptation.

We become extra careful during cleanup to ensure that no food particles remain in the dishes or land on the ground. All waste products go in the sump hole, which we cover with dirt for the night. Next we stow all the food, cooking utensils, dishes, toothpaste, and soap in duffels and haul everything over to the hanging site. It takes the three of us to hoist it.

DAY FOUR MENU

Breakfast

Flapjacks
Coffee

Trail Lunch

C. W.'s Turkey Jerky
Cracker Mix
Dates
Almond M&M's

Dinner

Rapid Trail
Boot Wax Apples

DAY FOUR

Pilgrims and pioneers relished the taste of griddle cakes made with what they called "Indian meal." Stirring up cornmeal, sour milk, saleratus (a kind of baking soda), and sugar, camp cooks would start flipping flapjacks before dawn to satisfy the hungry appetites of field hands. Because breakfast was often the only meal served as part of a hired hand's "room and board," women's journals recorded fixing the men twenty to thirty flapjacks apiece. One frustrated cook gave out after a worker came back for his seventy-fourth flapjack.

Day Four Breakfast Recipe

Flapjacks

1 1/2 c. cornmeal

1 c. flour

1 t. baking powder

1 t. salt

1/4 c. sugar

1/4 c. powdered milk

6 T. margarine

> *Bag together all ingredients except margarine.*

In-the-field preparation

> *Melt 3 T. margarine in the skillet. Add it and 1 c. cold water to bag of dry ingredients. Reseal and gently squeeze to moisten. Add more water if need. It should pour into the skillet as a thick batter. Melt enough of remaining margarine to lightly coat the bottom of the skillet. Pour in some batter, cover, and cook until tops are firm and undersides brown. Flip. Repeat until all batter is used. Makes 12–16, depending on size of cakes. Serve with molasses.*
>
> > **THIS MEAL** *requires no adaptation for any of the other types of trips.*

We camp opposite of Pingora Peak, the most prominent formation in the Cirque of the Tower. It ranks as a favorite for ambitious climbers, shooting up from Lonesome Lake like a gargantuan tree stump. Supposedly, Pingora derives its name from the Shoshone language and means "high, rocky inaccessible peak."

We break camp and zigzag back down Jackass Pass, stopping on the shore of North Lake again to lunch among the boulders, sheltered from the ever-present wind—one of the elements the Cheyenne used in drying jerky. After cutting meat into thin strips, the women laid the pieces over bushes or on a hide, letting the sun

and air draw the moisture out of the meat. (The chore of keeping bugs and other things away from the meat fell on the children.) Once the meat dehydrated, the women packed it in parfleches, boxes made from heavy buffalo rawhide convenient for packing on a horse's back.

Day Four Trail Lunch Recipe

C. W.'s Turkey (or Chicken) Jerky
1 lb. boned turkey (or chicken breast)
   sliced thin
1/4 c. soy sauce
1 t. garlic Powder
1 t. salt

1 t. onion powder
1 t. ginger
1 t. chili powder
1 t. basil
1 t. ground coriander seed

Partially freeze meat. Cut into thin strips. Mix together remaining ingredients. Lay strips of fowl in a glass 9 x 13 inch pan. Spoon seasoning mixture evenly over meat. Repeat with another layer. Cover with plastic wrap. Marinate 24 hours. Spread on foil-lined oven rack and dehydrate.

A yellow-bellied marmot scurries out of his burrow in the rock slide and onto his observation platform, which happens to be just above our picnic area. From this pedestal, the furry little lookout scolds us for intruding. Dick gets a good picture of the marmot that keeps a wary eye on Jeff and me as we refill our water bottles for the next leg of the journey.

It's midafternoon by the time we reach Rapid Creek Trail, which leads us to our second destination, East Temple Peak. The trail weaves among tall pines that obstruct the view of the stream running out of Rapid Lake. Sounds of gushing water meander in and out of hearing range as we progress up the steep incline.

We reach its plateau near Miller Lake and take a water break. I seize the opportunity to slip into a sweater and pull pants over my shorts, feeling the chill produced by the higher altitude. For every one thousand feet in elevation, the temperature drops three to six degrees. A strong wind chill makes it colder still.

Even though it's been a long day, we decide to travel a bit farther. Jeff passes around some dried pineapple, known to hikers as "power rings" as they provide a quick boost of energy. Meanwhile, I add water to tonight's zucchini. By the time we make camp, we'll be waving the hunger handkerchief—a practice of early American farm hands to signal their need for food.

Beyond Miller Lake, the trail slants upward very gently toward Temple Lake, actually three connecting bodies of water. Rays of the setting sun shimmer on the distant snow-frosted peaks by the time we locate a small depression in the slope above the lower end of the lake. Darkness casts its shadow as we set up our base camp at 10,600 feet elevation.

Stunted limber pines maintain a meager hold on this snow-dappled pocket of soil. Dick and Jeff anchor our fly to the sturdy tree limbs the same way the indigenous peoples of the plains tied a cloth or hide canopy between trees for protection from the elements.

I arrange packs around a rock outcropping to form a windshield for the kitchen area. Home for two nights!

Our appetite hardly allows us to wait for the cheese to melt over the zucchini and cracker mixture. Crackers, and their harder, heavier counterpart hardtack, graced many a pioneer meal. Oregon Trail traveler Ellen Toole wrote in her diary, "Had ham, dried beef, crackers, pickle, and syrup for dinner with brandy today." Many women baked a supply of crackers before leaving for the West and packed them in boxes for the trip. They made them by combining a pound of flour, a pinch each of cream of tartar and saleratus, and two ounces of fresh butter with enough milk to form a stiff paste. Next the women beat the mixture smooth with a rolling pin then rolled the dough out very thin. After cutting the crackers in squares and pricking each with a fork, the cook transferred the squares to a cookie tin and baked them in a hot oven.

Day Four Dinner Recipes

Rapid Trail

4 medium zucchini, sliced thin

2 onions, diced

1 bell pepper, chopped

1 c. swiss cheese, grated

12 mushrooms, sliced

1 pimento pepper, chopped

1 t. cayenne pepper

1 t. black pepper

16 saltine crackers, crushed

1/4 c. margarine

Dehydrate zucchini, onions, and peppers. Bag vegetables together. Crush crackers and bag with cayenne and black pepper. Bag cheeses separately.

Boot Wax Apples

2 apples

1/3 c. sugar

1 t. cinnamon

1 pkg. instant butterscotch pudding mix

1/3 c. powdered milk

Dehydrate apples and bag with the sugar and cinnamon. Bag pudding mix and powdered milk together.

In-the-field preparation

Rehydrate vegetables and apples. Collect small bowls and lids while water boils for hot drinks. Place vegetables in the skillet. Cover. Bring to a boil over high heat. Reduce to medium and cook until tender. Once done, shove vegetables to one side of the skillet. Add margarine. When it has melted, blend in crackers and vegetables. Add cheese and more margarine if needed. Mix thoroughly. Cover and remove from heat. Serve when cheese has melted.

While eating dinner, cook apples in sugar, cinnamon, and 1/4 c. water until it cooks down. Divide pudding mix evenly between the bowls. Add 1/2 c. of cold water per container. Cover and shake for 30 seconds. Allow pudding to sit for 5 minutes. Pour apples over pudding and serve.

***AS AN OPTION** on float trips and car camping, substitute fresh vegetables and store in an ice chest. Otherwise, this meal is suitable as is for other types of trips.*

DAY FIVE MENU

Breakfast
Orange Sunrise
Pemmican
Coffee

Trail Lunch
Jerky Pingora Style
Cheese
Triscuits
Pineapple and Papaya Chunks
Mixed Nuts
Caramels
M&M's

Dinner
Summit
Hiker's Heaven
Cold Night Hot Toddy

DAY FIVE

The morning to ascend East Temple Peak arrives, demanding a hearty, stick-with-you breakfast that begins with pemmican. Indigenous peoples shared this recipe with settlers as a means of preserving meat and berries in a nutritious, tasty manner. Cheyenne women pounded dried meat with a stone maul on a flat rock that rested in the bottom of a dish-shaped parfleche; as the meat powdered, they add dried berries. Once this step was completed, the women removed the stone and poured melted fat and sometimes bone marrow over the mixture and served it.

Day Five Breakfast Recipes

Orange Sunrise

2 c. flour

1/2 c. sugar

2 t. salt

2 t. allspice

2 t. baking powder

2 t. dried orange peel

4 T. orange drink mix

1/2 c. powdered milk

1/2 c. plus 1 T. margarine

Bag all ingredients together, except margarine.

Orange Glaze

1/4 c. powdered sugar

1 T. margarine

Bag separately.

Pemmican

1 lb. ground meat

1 pt. raspberries

4 T. margarine

Brown the ground meat. Dehydrate it and the berries. When dry, grind to a powder in a blender. Store in zipper plastic bag separate from the margarine.

In-the-field preparation

Melt 1 /2 c. margarine in the skillet. Mix in 1/2 c. cold water. Add margarine mixture to dry Orange Sunrise ingredients. Reseal and squeeze gently until ingredients are completely moistened and mixture makes a stiff dough. Melt 1 T. margarine in the skillet, swirling to coat the bottom and sides. Pat dough into skillet. Cover and bake over low heat with lid fire for 50 minutes.

Put 4 T. margarine in the small pan. Hold over the lid fire until margarine melts.
Remove from heat and add pemmican powder and mix well. Divide among the bowls and
serve while the Orange Sunrise bakes. Melt 1 T. margarine in a small pan and hold over
lid fire. When melted, pour into sugar. Reseal bag and squeeze to mix. Drizzle over hot
rolls. Cut into wedges and serve.

THIS MEAL requires no adaptation to be suitable for any other types of trips.

Before we load our day packs with trail foods and plenty of water, I start the rehydration process on the chicken and vegetables. We'll be in need of a fast dinner tonight.

We skirt the upper sections of Temple Lake, locked in ice. Beyond it lays a nearly vertical snowfield up the mountainside. Jeff shows Dick and me how to "kick step" our way up it by cutting into the snow with the toe and side of our boot. This creates a platform to stand on while we cut the next step. It sounds easy, but within half an hour my calves, as well as my lungs, protest vigorously. Pausing, I lean into the slope and try to catch my breath. Then I push on. Time is working against us. We need to reach the summit before noon because once the sun hits this snowfield head-on, softening it, travel might become tricky, possibly even dangerous.

Exertion mixed with the warming day already sees us shedding our fleecy pile jackets and pants. By the second hour, fatigue sets in. Jeff heads for a patch of snow-free, boulder-cluttered ground. Springs flow and pool up in clusters of rock, ready-made fountains for our water bottles. Reclining against boulders, we energize our bodies with extra rations of trail foods. The pineapple, caramels, and M&M's receive the bulk of our attention. But the sun continues to climb toward the zenith. So must we. Light radiates scorching brightness off the snow as we get closer to our destination. The surface soon turns slick and a bit slushy beneath our boots. Near the top, the snow gives way to huge boulders precariously scattered. A stout air current blows up and over the summit. When I crawl up onto the rock at the very pinnacle of East Temple Peak, elevation 12,590 feet, a quote from a James Cagney movie leaps instantly to mind: "Top of the world, Ma!" From the summit, the heart of the Winds' high peaks, forty-three of them over 12,500 feet, commandeer the horizon. A truly awesome sight.

The ascent took over four hours. We descend in less than half that time and in a far more enjoyable manner, too. Mountaineers call it "glissading." With feet together, we squat and push off with our hands, sliding down snowfields with our hiking boots doubling for a sled. Of course, we amateurs all end up on our bottoms. And at one point, Dick careens out of control, rumbling over me, practically slamming into a boulder and winds up spinning around like a break-dancer imitating an upside-down turtle! What a day!

Day Five Dinner Recipes

Summit

3 chicken breasts, ground

2 onions

1 20 oz pkg. frozen stir-fry vegetables

6 mushrooms

1 t. garlic powder

1 t. ginger

1 chicken bouillon cube

1 t. cornstarch

1 T. margarine

2 1/2 c. chow mien noodles

2 T. soy sauce

Dehydrate chicken, mushrooms, stir-fry vegetables, and onions. Bag these together with bouillon cube (remove wrapper), garlic powder, and ginger. Keep cornstarch, noodles, margarine, and soy sauce all separate.

Hiker's Heaven

1 12 oz. bag of semisweet chocolate chips

1/2 c. coconut flakes

1/2 c. slivered almond

1/2 t. Chinese five-spice

1 c. chow mein noodles

Bag chocolate, coconut, nuts, and spice together. Store noodles separately.

Cold Night Hot Toddy

1 c. powdered milk

1 T. nutmeg

4 T margarine

Bag milk and nutmeg together and separate from margarine.

In-the-field preparation

Reconstitute chicken and vegetables by adding a cup more of water than it takes to cover everything. Make a hot drink. Melt margarine in skillet. Pour chicken mixture into skillet, ensuring that there is a full cup of liquid. Cover. Bring to a boil over high heat. Reduce to low and simmer until meat and vegetables are tender. Add water if needed to maintain a cup of liquid. Mix cornstarch, soy sauce, and 1/4 c. water in a plastic bag and set aside. When food is done, check fluid level and bring to a boil once again. Add cornstarch mixture. Cook 1 minute, stirring constantly. Serve over chow mein noodles. For dessert, melt chocolate mixture over low heat in pan. Collect the smaller bowls. When chocolate melts, stir in noodles. Divide among the bowls. Serve. When ready to round off the evening, boil 4 c water. Stir in milk mixture and margarine. Serve.

AS AN OPTION on float trips and car camping, substitute fresh chicken that has been frozen and frozen stir-fry vegetables, provided this meal is served within the first two days of the voyage. Otherwise, substitute canned chicken, which makes this meal suitable for goat and horse trips as well.

DAY SIX MENU

Breakfast

Windpants

Coffee

Trail Lunch

Cashews

Pumpkin Seeds

Banana Chips

Cracker Mix

Licorice

Dinner

Hiking Hollandaise

Jerky

Day's End Cake

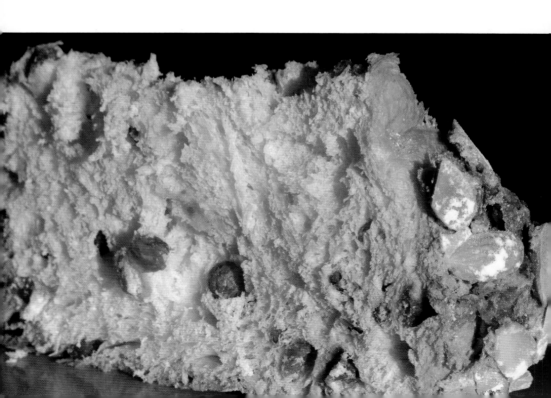

DAY SIX

Day Six Breakfast Recipes

Windpants

4 pears, sliced thin

1 t. cinnamon

1 t. cayenne pepper

1 t. mace

1 t. nutmeg

1/2 c. brown sugar, packed firm

1 recipe of Mountain Baking Mix

Dry pear slices and bag. Mix remaining ingredients together and bag.

Mountain Baking Mix

1 1/2 c. flour

1 T. baking powder

3 T. powdered milk

1 t. salt

Mix and bag.

In-the-field preparation

Fill a large pot half full of cold water. Add pears-and-brown-sugar mix. Cover and bring to a boil over high heat. Add 1 1/4 c. cold water to the Mountain Baking Mix to make a stiff dough. Reseal the bag and squeeze it between your fingers until completely mixed. Drop dough a teaspoon at a time into the boiling pears. Lower heat and simmer covered, for 30 minutes.

__AS AN OPTION__ on any of the other kinds of trips, substitute fresh or canned pears.

Day Six Dinner Recipes

Hiking Hollandaise

1 lb. broccoli flower heads, broken into small pieces

1 onion, chopped

12 mushrooms, sliced thin

4 stalks celery, chopped

3 c. vegetable noodles

2 1.6 oz pkg. Hollandaise Sauce Mix

Remove stems from broccoli flowers. Dehydrate along with onion, mushrooms, and celery. (Stems take much longer to rehydrate, slowing the cooking process if included.) Bag together. Bag noodles separately. Don't forget to include the 2 pkg. of sauce mix.

Day's End Cake

1 1/3 c. whole wheat flour

2/3 c. powdered sugar

1 t. salt

2/3 c. dates

1/3 c. almond slivers

1 t. cream of tartar

1/4 c. brown sugar

1 t. baking powder

1/2 c. margarine

Mix all ingredients except margarine in a zipper bag.

In-the-field preparation

Rehydrate vegetables by filling half the bag with cold water. Once everybody has a hot drink, pour the soaking broccoli mixture into the pot. Cover and bring to a boil over high heat. Reduce to medium heat and cook until vegetables are tender 20–30 minutes. Stir frequently. Add more water as needed to keep vegetables covered. When broccoli mixture is cooked, add enough water to cover ingredients again (if necessary) and bring back to boil over high heat. Add noodles. Cook, covered, over medium heat until noodles are done, about 10 minutes more. Stir frequently. If there isn't a cup of liquid in the vegetable/noodle mixture, add more. Sprinkle sauce mix into ingredients. Cook, stirring constantly until sauce thickens. Remove from heat. Melt 1/2 c. margarine in the skillet. Add it and 1 c. water to dry cake ingredients. Mix until you have a thick batter. Pour into the skillet. Cover. Bake over low heat and a lid fire for 20–40 minutes or until done.

__AS AN OPTION__ on float trips or car camping, take fresh or frozen broccoli and fresh mushrooms and celery in the ice chest. For goat and horse trips, follow the recipe unless this meal will be prepared the first night.

DAY SEVEN MENU

Breakfast

Packframe Potato Cakes

Fruit and Nuts

Coffee

Trail Lunch

C. W.'s jerky

Pineapple Rings

Walnuts

Cracker Mix

Assorted M&M's

Dinner

Ditty Bag

Wilderness Strawberry Cheesecake

Tea

DAY SEVEN

Day Seven Breakfast Recipe

Packframe Potato Cakes
1 c. flour
1 c. instant potatoes
1 c. powdered milk
1 1/2 t. baking powder

2 t. salt
1/2 t. cayenne
1/4 lb. cheese, sliced
1/4 c. margarine

Mix together all ingredients except cheese and margarine, which are bagged separately. Store in plastic bag.

In-the-field preparation

While coffee water boils, pour 1 1/2 c. cold water into the bag of dry Packframe Potato Cake ingredients. Reseal bag and gently squeeze it in your hands until well blended. This will resemble a thick batter. Add more water if necessary. Melt enough margarine in the skillet to coat the bottom. Spoon batter into pan, forming small pancakes. Cover. Cook over low heat until cake bottoms are brown and the tops firm. Flip. Add more margarine if needed. Lay a slice of cheese on top. Cover and cook until the bottoms brown and cheese are melted. While cakes are cooking, pull out a bag of dried fruit and nuts to serve with them.

THIS MEAL requires no adaptation for other types of trips unless you care to serve fresh fruits instead of dried.

Day Seven Dinner Recipes

Ditty Bag

1 1/2 lbs. ground beef
12 mushrooms, sliced thin
1 10 oz. pkg. frozen peas
4 large carrots, sliced

1 onion, chopped
3 c. egg noodles
1 recipe sauce mix

Bag together all ingredients except egg noodles and sauce mix, which are bagged separately.

Sauce Mix

1/2 c. flour	**1** T. dry mustard
1/2 c. powdered milk	**1** t. celery salt
1 T. black pepper	**1** t. thyme
1 t. cayenne pepper	**1** t. garlic powder
2 T. parsley flakes	**1** t. onion powder
2 t. salt	**1** t. chili powder

Mix together in a plastic bag. Keep sauce mix and egg noodles in separate bags.

Wilderness Strawberry Cheesecake

1 box of cheesecake mix	**12** graham crackers, crushed
1/2 pt. fresh strawberries, sliced thin then dehydrated	

Remove cheesecake mix from the box and pour into a plastic bag. In separate bags, store strawberries and crushed crackers.

In-the-field preparation

Rehydrate meat and vegetables. Do not add water to the noodles or sauce mix. Meanwhile, make tea and collect everybody's little bowl. Pour some of the crushed graham crackers into the bottom of each bowl. Add enough cold water to the cheesecake mix to completely moisten, squeezing gently to thoroughly blend. Spoon it over the crackers, dividing it evenly. Set aside. Pour the soaking meat and vegetables into the pot. Cover and bring to a boil over high heat. Reduce to medium heat and cook 20 minutes or until meat and vegetables are tender. Stir frequently. Add more water as needed to keep meat and vegetables covered.

To rehydrate strawberry slices, cover with cold water and set bag on top of the lid of the cooking Ditty Bag. If lid becomes too hot, remove strawberries. When the meat mixture is cooked, add enough water to cover ingredients again (if necessary) and bring to boil. Add noodles. Cook over medium heat until noodles are done, about 10 minutes. Stir frequently. Add additional water if needed to ensure 1/3 inch in the bottom of the pan. Add sauce mix, stirring constantly until water is absorbed by the sauce mix and it cooks for five minutes. If sauce become too thick, thin with a bit of cold water. Serve. During dinner, put a covered pot of water on to boil for another round of tea and for washup. When ready to serve cheesecake, spoon strawberries on top and hand out.

AS AN OPTION *goat and horse trips substitute canned vegetables. On float trip and car camping, fresh or frozen ground beef and fresh or frozen strawberries may be substituted if the meal is served within the first three days of the trip. Store in an ice chest.*

DAY EIGHT MENU

Breakfast

Boulder Field

Coffee

Trail Lunch

Jerky Pingora Style

Raisins

Assorted Fruit Leathers

Yogurt Balls

Dinner

Gaiters

Wild Side Rice

Trailblazer Biscuits

DAY EIGHT

Day Eight Breakfast Recipe

Boulder Field

4 c. Grape-Nuts

8 T. orange drink mix

1/3 c. powdered milk

1 c. chopped nuts

Bag all ingredients together.

In-the-field preparation

Gather large bowls while water boils for coffee. Divide dry ingredients into bowls; add enough water to gain consistency of cereal and milk. Serve.

THIS MEAL *requires no alteration for goat, horse, or float trips.*

Day Eight Dinner Recipes

Gaiters

1 eggplant, sliced thin

1 onion, chopped

8 mushrooms. sliced thin

4 tomatoes, chopped

1 t. pepper

1/2 t. garlic powder

1 t. basil

1 t. parsley flakes

1 recipe Wild Side Rice

Dry eggplant, onion, mushrooms, and tomatoes. Bag with seasonings. Store rice separately.

Trailblazer Biscuits

1 1/3 c. flour

1/3 c. sugar

1 t. salt

1 t. baking powder

1 t. baking soda

1 t. ground coriander seed

1/4 c. powdered milk

1/4 c. plus 2 T. margarine

Bag together all ingredients except margarine.

Strawberry Topping

1 pt. strawberries, sliced thin

1/4 c. powdered milk

Dehydrate strawberries and bag with milk.

Wild Side Rice

1 c. brown rice   **1** c. water

In a covered medium saucepan, bring rice and water to a boil. Add 1/3 c. more cold water. Simmer, covered, 30 minutes. When cooked, spread on foil-covered oven racks and dry.

In-the-field preparation

Rehydrate vegetables and Strawberry Topping. Put a pot of water on to boil. Collect large bowls. Divide rice between the four bowls. When water boils, pour 1/3 c. over each bowl of rice. Put the lids on and set aside. The rice needs at least 10–15 minutes to reconstitute. Place eggplant mixture and an additional 1 c. cold water in a large pot. Cover and bring to a boil over high heat. Reduce to low and simmer until tender. Serve over the rice. Cut 1/4 c. margarine into dry biscuit ingredients. Add l/3 c. cold water. Reseal bag and squeeze to mix. Makes a stiff dough. Pat balls of dough into biscuits no more than 1/2 inch thick.

Arrange in a skillet. Cover. Bake over low with a lid fire for 25–30 minutes. Serve with Strawberry Topping. Makes 12–15 biscuits.

__AS AN OPTION__ car camping or on float trips, substitute fresh vegetables and tomatoes and either fresh or frozen strawberries. If this will be the first evening's meal on goat or horse trip, fresh foods may be taken. Otherwise, use this recipe on animal-assisted trips.

DAY NINE MENU

Breakfast
Shorts
Coffee

Trail Lunch
Cheese

Assorted Crackers
Apricots
Cashews
M&Ms

Dinner
Tent Stake Turkey
Snow Drifts

DAY NINE

Day Nine Breakfast Recipe

Shorts

1 1/2 lb. ground beef
1 c. flour
1/3 c. buckwheat flour
1/3 c. Malt-O-Meal

1 t. baking powder
1 t. salt
5 T. powdered buttermilk
6 T. margarine
3 pkg. brown gravy mix

Brown meat. Dehydrate and bag. Bag together remaining ingredients except for margarine and gravy mix, which are stored in two separate bags.

In-the-field preparation

Rehydrate meat. While water boils for coffee, cut margarine into the shortcake mix. Add 3/4 c. water into the shortcake mixture. Seal bag and squeeze to moisten ingredients. Form biscuits about 1/2 inch thick. Drop into the skillet. Cover and bake with a lid fire for 25–30 minutes. Makes 20. When done, remove and set aside. In smaller pot, bring meat and enough water to cover the bottom of the pan to a boil over high heat. Cook, adding more water if necessary, until meat is tender. Add 3 c. of cold water and the gravy mix. Bring to a boil over low heat, stirring constantly. Boil for three minutes. Serve over shortcakes.

AS AN OPTION *car camping or on float trips, substitute frozen ground meat stored in an ice chest. For goat and horse trips, use the frozen meat alternative only if this breakfast will be your first in the field.*

Day Nine Dinner Recipes

Tent Stake Turkey

2 lb. ground turkey

1 onion

4 stalks celery

1 20 oz. pkg. frozen green beans (or 1 lb. fresh)

1 box cornbread stuffing mix

1 pkg. turkey gravy mix

1/4 c. margarine

Dehydrate turkey, onion, beans, and celery. Do not thaw beans first. Bag meat and vegetables with the stuffing seasoning packet. Store stuffing bread, margarine, and gravy mix in three separate bags.

Snow Drifts

1/4 c. cornstarch

3/4 c. coconut

1/2 t. cinnamon

1/4 c. powdered milk

1 t. salt

3/4 c. sugar

1/3 c. raisins (optional)

Mix together and bag.

In-the-field preparation

Reconstitute meat-and-vegetable mixture. Make hot drinks. Put meat mixture in the large pot. Cover and bring to a boil over high heat. Add water as it becomes absorbed. Pour pudding mix into a large pot. Slowly stir in 1 1/4 c. water. Cook over medium heat until mixture boils, stirring constantly. Boil 3 minutes. This is very rich!

__AS AN OPTION__ car camping or on float trips, substitute frozen turkey and beans and fresh celery and onion. Keep the recipe as is for goat and horse trips unless it will be served the first night.

DAY TEN MENU

Breakfast

Cirques

Coffee

Trail Lunch

C. W.'s jerky

Corn Nuts

Dates

Summer Season Fruit Mix

Caramels

Dinner

Rocky Mountain Trout

Moleskin Mushroom Soup

Mediterranean Vegetable Mix

Camp Comfort

DAY TEN

Day Ten Breakfast Recipe

Cirques

4 slices ham, ground
1 10 oz. pkg. frozen corn
2 c. flour
2 t. baking powder

2 t. salt
1/2 c. powdered milk
4 T. margarine

Dehydrate ham and corn. NOTE: do not use popcorn instead. Popcorn makes a poor substitute for sweet corn. Also, don't thaw corn before drying. Just arrange it and the ham on foil-lined oven racks. Bag together all remaining ingredients except margarine.

In-the-field preparation

Rehydrate ham and corn. Double-decker the bag containing ham mixture on the lid while making coffee. Pour ham mixture in the skillet and bring to a boil over high heat. Add 2 c. cold water to flour mix. Squeeze in the bag to completely moisten, making a thick batter. Add ham mixture. Melt 1 T. margarine in the skillet. Spoon fritters into it and cook, covered, over medium heat. Flip once. Repeat until all batter is used. If the outside is cooking too fast while the middle stays raw, reduce heat. Makes 20. Serve with honey if desired.

AS AN OPTION car camping or on float trips, take fresh, frozen, or canned ham and corn. Canned foods work well on the goat and horse trips.

Day Ten Trail Lunch Recipe

Summer Season Fruit Mix

1/2 cantaloupe, diced
1/2 honeydew melon, diced
2 c. blueberries

1 pt. strawberries, sliced thin
6 peaches, pitted and sliced thin

Dehydrate. Mix together and bag for the trail. NOTE: honeydew melon makes a delicious addition to trail food; however, when reconstituted, the flavor washes out.

AS AN OPTION car camping or on float trips, use fresh fruits. The recipe remains as is for goat and horse trips.

Day Ten Dinner Recipes

Rocky Mountain Trout

1 trout, cleaned (per person)   **4** slices of lemon
1/4 c. onion, chopped

> Dehydrate onion and lemon. Bag together. NOTE: if you don't plan to fish on your trip, or doubt your luck, bring along a spare dehydrated meal from the goat packing or horse packing sections.

Moleskin Mushroom Soup

1 onion, chopped   **4** slices whole wheat bread
6 mushrooms, sliced   **3** T. margarine
3 beef bouillon cubes   **2** T. Parmesan cheese

> Dehydrate onion, mushrooms, and bread slices. Bag onion, mushrooms, and bouillon cubes (remove wrappers) together. Store margarine, bread, and cheese in three separate bags.

Mediterranean Vegetable Mix

1 1/3 20 oz. bags of frozen mixed garden vegetables

> *Spread on foil-covered oven racks and dry. No need to thaw first.*

Camp Comfort

1 3 oz. pkg. raspberry flavored gelatin mix   **1** t. cinnamon

> *Remove gelatin from the box and bag with cinnamon.*

In-the-field preparation

Rehydrate onion/lemon mixture and the onion/mushroom mixture. Make hot drinks in a large pot, ensuring 2 c. of water remain. Add onion/mushroom mixture. Cover and bring to a boil over high heat. Reduce to medium and cook until vegetables are tender. Pour soup into large bowls. Float a piece of bread on top of each portion. Sprinkle with cheese and serve. Eat while preparing the fish and vegetables. Bring vegetables and enough water to cover them to boil in the smaller pot over high heat. Simmer until the fish is ready to cook. Stuff onion in trout. Lay lemon slices on top. Add 1 c. cold water. Cover and steam in the skillet 30–35 minutes. Flip fish once about halfway through cooking time. Add more water if necessary. Employ the double-decker method to keep the vegetables hot while the trout cooks. When it starts to boil, reduce to low heat and simmer until meat and vegetables are tender (approximately 20 minutes, depending on altitude). Serve.

Heat more water. Collect mugs. Spoon 2 T. of gelatin mix in each mug and add boiling water. Stir well and serve.

***AS AN OPTION** for car camping or on goat, horse, or float trips, bring canned fish as a substitute for fresh trout and a fresh lemon. A raw onion and canned mushrooms and beef broth can replace the dried soup ingredients. A mix of fresh or frozen vegetables can replace dried on a float trip, but stick to the dehydrated ones on goat and horse trips unless they will be served the first night.*

CHAPTER TWO

SEVEN DAYS ON HORSEBACK HAULIN' PANNIERS

The tradition of horse packing in the American West dates back to not long after Plains Nations captured the first wild horses. Like these tribes, explorers, mountain men, and miners adopted horse packing as a way of life. Nowadays, outfitters continue the practice of this ancient custom.

Horse-packing excursions come in many forms. Guest ranches often include horse-packing treks as part of the vacation package. These last anywhere from overnight to several days in the field. Then there's completely outfitted expeditions which the whole family, including very small children, can enjoy together. Most outfitters provide full-service horse trips with hired cooks and wranglers who care for the animals in the field and do all the loading, unloading, setting up, and breaking down of camp. Some outfitters, however, do offer hands-on trips for do-it-yourselfers. Both of these types of horse-packing ventures can last a week or more. Therefore here are seven days' worth of meals suitable for horse-packing adventures.

FOOD ON THE TRAIL

Horse packing provides days of perpetual motion. It isn't fair to horses or mules loaded down with 100 to 150 pounds to stand around while humans stop for lunch, so you'll usually consume trail foods while riding rather than taking breaks. Think of your saddlebags as lunch boxes on horseback. They protect the food and keep it readily accessible. Bagels, sandwiches with cheese and hard salami or summer sausage, fresh fruit, candy or granola bars all work well for horse-borne midday meals. Or choose from the list of sandwich fillers below.

As with goat packing, keep in mind the horse hauls the weight, therefore a standard workday or school day lunch like a bagel, some salami, cheese, and a piece of fruit will adequately satisfy the appetite. Horse-packing lunches fall closer to one-quarter pound per person per day.

SANDWICH FILLERS

- Cheddar cheese grated with chopped sweet pickle, and chili sauce
- Saddle Bags Chicken Spread (see recipe below)
- Cold cuts with chinese hot mustard
- Corned beef hash and horseradish
- Crab Pardner (see recipe below)
- Dates chopped with almonds
- Deviled ham and chopped dill pickles
- Hard salami with sliced cheddar and horseradish
- Peanut butter and chopped prunes
- Peanut butter with banana chips
- Sardine Sling (see recipe below)
- Parmesan Half Hitch (see recipe below)
- Hot Carrot Spread (see recipe below)

EXTRAS FOR THE TRAIL:

A plastic bottle of soy sauce, Worcestershire sauce, honey, molasses, salt, and pepper.

SUPPLY LIST (7 DAYS)

Baking Staples

1 10 oz. box baking powder
1 lb. brown sugar
1 lb. buckwheat flour
1 16 oz. box cornstarch
1 25.6 oz. box powdered milk
1 16 oz. can powdered buttermilk

1 26 oz. box salt
5 lb. sack flour
1 18 oz. box oats
5 lb. sack sugar
1 lb. whole wheat flour

Canned Goods

1 16 oz. can apricots in juice
1 14 oz. can bean sprouts
1 5 oz. can chicken
1 6 oz. can crab meat
2 10 3/4 oz. cans cream of asparagus soup

1 10 1/2 oz. can cream of mushroom soup
2 16 oz. cans fruit cocktail in juice
2 15 1/2 oz. cans kidney beans
1 11 oz can Mandarin orange segments
1 16 oz. can sliced peaches in juice

1 20 oz. can pineapple chunks in juice
2 14 3/4 oz. cans salmon
1 7 oz. can Salsa Verde

2 3 3/4 oz. cans sardines in mustard
1 15 oz. can corned beef hash

Crackers/Cereals/Breads

1 15 oz. box crisp rice cereal
1 lb. box graham crackers
2 large flour tortillas
1 10 oz. bag pretzels

1 lb. box saltine crackers
1 loaf sliced bread
8 whole wheat flour tortillas

Dried Fruit /Vegetables /Nuts

1 c. mixed dried fruit
1/4 c. nuts
1/3 c. pecans

1 lb. box raisins
2 2 oz. pkg. almond slivers
2 8 oz. boxes pitted dates

Fresh Fruit

2 apples
1 cantaloupe
1 watermelon

bags of mixed fruit (1/4 lb. per person, per day)

Fresh Vegetables

3 bell peppers
3 carrots
2 cloves garlic
2 eggplants
1 head cabbage

22 mushrooms
6 onions
5 potatoes
1 bunch celery
6 tomatoes

Frozen Food

1 16 oz. pkg. frozen broccoli
2 16 oz. pkg frozen corn

1 16 oz. pkg. frozen peas
1 16 oz. pkg. frozen peas and carrots

Meat /Milk/Margarine/Cheese/Eggs

16 eggs
1 lb. bag egg noodles
1 8 oz. container Parmesan cheese
1/2 lb. cheese
1/2 lb. swiss cheese
1 lb. summer sausage

5 chicken franks
1 4.5 oz. jar dried beef
2 lbs. ground beef
2 lbs. sausage
1 lb. margarine

Rice/Noodles

1 16 oz. bag spinach noodles

Sauce & Other Mixes/Drinks/Specialty Items

1 20 oz. can hot chocolate mix

1 14 oz. bag caramels

1 bottle catsup

1 plastic jar chunky peanut butter

1 8 oz. container cocoa

1 2.9 oz. box custard mix

1 bottle honey

1 jar horseradish

1 jar Hot English Mustard

1 bottle reconstituted lemon juice

1 jar mayonnaise

1 bottle molasses

1 bottle soy sauce

1 bottle Tabasco

1 bottle vinegar

1 1.5 oz. pkg. white sauce mix

1 bottle Worcestershire sauce

assorted flavors of fruit crystals

60 assorted tea bags and coffee (optional)

Spices

1 container allspice

1 container basil

1 container caraway seed

1 container cayenne pepper

1 container chili powder

1 container cinnamon

1 container dry mustard

1 container garlic powder

1 container hickory smoke salt

1 container nutmeg

1 container onion powder

1 container paprika

1 container parsley flakes

1 container pepper

LUNCHES

Choose from the list in sandwich fillers, spread on bagels, bread, rolls, tortillas, or muffins. Also take along fresh fruit for on the trail. (About 1/4 pound per person per day.)

DAY ONE MENU

Breakfast

Irish Canyon Eggs

Coffee

Trail Lunch

Cheddar cheese grated with chopped sweet pickle

Chili sauce

Saddle Bags Chicken Spread

Fresh fruit

Dinner

Mule Meatloaf

Rumpstrap

Panniers Pecan Delight

Tea

DAY ONE

Frost glitters in the mid-June sunshine as we unload horses and gear at the Irish Canyon road head in Wyoming's Wind River Range. The two horses and one mule we'll be packing with on this trip belong to Teri. She invited us to bring our horses and join her on a test run for Smoke, Blaze, and Sandy the mule, the latest additions to the herd Teri started for her outfitting business. Kirk and Joy, Teri's brother and sister-in-law, take a matched pair of chestnuts named Dancer and Prancer out of the trailer. Kirk's buddy Alex leads his paint, nicknamed Pain (short for Pain-in-the-Neck), to a line of pines at the edge of the parking lot and ties Pain to a tree trunk near the other horses while I unload Onyx.

Although Teri asked me to coordinate the rations on this informal trip, we'll take turns cooking. So once we grain the horses and mule, the others make sandwiches and pack the lunches in our saddle bags while I prepare a road head breakfast of Irish Canyon Eggs. In spring, the Cheyenne gathered large quantities of wild fowl eggs to supplement their diet. When white settlers crossed these mountains, heading for the West Coast, some brought preserved eggs with them. The pioneers greased the shells of raw eggs with melted mutton or pork fat then packed them tightly in a box filled with bran, straw, or ashes. Eggs, thus saved, lasted up to three months.

Day One Breakfast Recipe

Irish Canyon Eggs

10 mushrooms. sliced thin

1/2 onion, diced

1 14 oz. can bean sprouts

6 eggs

2 T. powdered milk

1 t. salt

1/2 t. cayenne pepper

Dehydrate mushrooms and onion. Bag them with the powdered milk, salt, and pepper.

In-the-field preparation

Rehydrate mushroom and onion by pouring the can of bean sprouts into them. Reseal and set aside. Make coffee. Pour mushroom mixture into the skillet. Cover. Bring to boil over medium heat. Beat eggs and add to mushroom mixture. Scramble over medium heat until done.

THIS MEAL needs no adaptation for car camping, float, or goat trips. For backpacking, this is only suitable for a first day meal, provided you don't mind the extra weight caused by the eggs and canned goods. (Powdered eggs just don't taste good enough to be an adequate substitute.)

Day One Lunch Recipe

Saddle Bag Chicken Spread

1 5 oz. can chicken   **2** T. honey

1/3 c. pecans, chopped   **1** T. lemon juice

Pack each item separately.

In-the-field preparation

Open chicken. Pour into the bag of nuts. Add remaining ingredients. Reseal bag and squeeze gently to mix. Spread on bread, bagels, or muffins.

THIS MEAL is suitable as is for car camping, goat, and float trips.

Back in 1859, Randolph Marcy wrote in his book, *The Prairie Traveler*, "It is no uncommon thing for them cruel masters to load their mules with the enormous burden of three or four hundred pounds." Nowadays, accepted carrying capacity ranges between 10 and 15 percent of the animal's total body weight, which translates into 100 to 150 pounds. Therefore panniers (saddlebags for pack animals) should weigh in the neighborhood of sixty pounds each, which allows for a top load in the form of a sack of grain, hay pellets, or sleeping bags. And don't forget, you have to heft those panniers up onto the pack saddle riding high on a tall horse! Teri uses a sawbuck, a popular style of pack saddle that can trace its origins back to a design developed by the indigenous peoples of the Plains Nations. Where they utilized the forks of a deer's or elk's antlers, modern sawbucks have wooden front and back cross-pieces in the shape of an X that the panniers hang from.

Unless you're hauling a bunch of extras such as wall tents, cots, or even portable bathtubs, one horse (or mule) can carry all the gear for two people. Since we have three pack animals and only five people, there's room for a two-burner stove, a folding table for the camp kitchen, cast iron dutch oven, and battery-operated lanterns (all plastic except for the light bulbs).

Carrying food on horse-packing trips requires some special wrapping and packing to keep things from rattling inside the panniers and spooking the pack animal. I double bag every recipe. Margarine goes in a plastic container with a screw-on lid, and that gets put in a zipper bag. (Ruptured margarine containers make a greasy mess.) Old-timers used to store eggs in their flour sacks or pancake mix. I prefer wrapping each egg in toilet paper, placing it in the hard plastic carton designed for carrying eggs into the backcountry. The eggs go on top of everything else in the pannier. Right under the eggs, I pack the first night's dinner ingredients so I won't have to dig for them when it comes time to eat. All nonperishable foods for each meal get packed into a cardboard box, stuffed with enough newspapers to keep items from shifting when you shake the box, then taped shut and labeled. I also mark on the outside of the box the amounts and types of perishable food that go with this meal.

Unless you view kerosene or stove gas as that special ingredient that adds zest to your meals, don't pack them in the same panniers with the food. Of course, if you're only packing with one horse, place the fuel bottles in the bottom of the pannier toward the back end (the horse's, that is). If the horse crashes into a tree and the fuel bottles happen to be in the front of the pannier, they could rupture and ruin everything. Pack all the food on the top so it rides high and centered on the horse, thus keeping it safe from the fuel. Additionally, glass bottles should be avoided. If broken, both you and your horse could be picking slivers out for days!

Alex helps me stow the breakables and perishables in rawhide panniers, plywood boxes that have been covered with cowhide, hair side out to keep them from rubbing sores on the horse. These rigid-sided panniers offer more protection for fragile contents when an animal decides it can squeeze between two trees that aren't quite wide enough to accommodate horse and pack load. Once we balance each set of panniers for equal weight, we hoist them on the sawbucks, cover them with a canvas manti (tarp) and secure the load by tying a basket hitch around everything. By late morning, we hit the trail.

We carry lunches in our saddlebags, eating as we ride rather than stopping for a meal. Even those "cruel masters" Marcy mentioned journeyed without "nooning" as nineteenth-century travelers called it, however, not for the same reason. "If the mules are suffered to halt," Marcy logged, "they are apt to lie down, and it is very difficult for them, with their loads, to rise; besides, they are likely to strain themselves in their efforts to do so." As for us, we simply believe it isn't fair to the animals to make them bear the pack weights while we humans take a break.

During the afternoon, we do make a couple of stops to adjust the order of the pack string. Sandy won't behave unless she leads. Blaze dislikes bringing up the rear. On the other hand, Smoke, an easygoing gray, doesn't seem to care where Teri puts him. Unfortunately, Boulderdash, the big Morgan she rides, takes exception when Sandy starts nipping Boulderdash's tail. Each time Teri disciplines the mule, Sandy lays her ears back, pouts, and slows up until it forces Teri to practically drag her along for a while. But none of the animals rodeo (the equivalent of equine kickboxing), so we declare the day a success. Later we amble into a medium-sized meadow filled with wildflowers and tall grasses. A creek gurgles nearby, an inviting sound. Birds chatter in the cluster of pines that ring the field. A perfect place to set up camp. As with goat packing, the first order of business is to tend to the animals. Untying the basket hitches, we remove the loads, mantis, panniers, and sawbucks. Next we give the animals a good brushing and lead them to the creek for a long drink.

Sir William Drummond Stewart hired a young artist named Alfred Jacob Miller to make on-the-spot sketches of the scenery and events of his expedition to what people in 1837 called the Far West, which included this area of the Wind River Range. Along with his drawings and watercolors, Miller kept a journal. In one entry, he noted asking permission to pay another member of the party to tend to his horse in the evenings. Stewart refused on the ground it would be a "breach of discipline and favoritism." So Miller sketched a picture he labeled *Picketing Horses*. The method has changed little since the notation that accompanied the drawing. Each man

caught his horse "by the lariat (a rope trailing on the ground from his neck), and leads him to a good bed of grass, where a picket is driven, and here he is secured for the night, the lariat permitting him to graze to the extent of a circle twenty-five feet in diameter."

We use a rope with a leather belt on one end that is buckled around the horse's front hoof instead of attaching it to his halter because it's very easy for a horse to get a foot tangled in a halter and hurt itself. The thirty-foot rope's other end is attached to a corkscrew-shaped rod we twist into the ground rather than pound in. Thus we stake out Boulderdash and Prancer, the dominant horses in the group. We hobble the rest (two leather belts with a short section of chain between them that is buckled to both front pasterns). Sandy, being the leader of the pack string, also gets a bell around her neck, something she is less than thrilled with. Last, we distribute some alfalfa pellets for all the horses to munch on along with the meadow grass. Then we fix and eat our mule meatloaf, not made from the real thing like it was in the nineteenth century. During what turned into a fifty-two-day "starvation march" on a campaign against the seven bands of the Tetons and Northern Cheyenne in 1876, calvary soldiers under General George Crook's command stayed alive until a detachment returned with supplies by boiling and roasting their pack mules.

Day One Dinner Recipes

Mule Meatloaf

1 lb. ground beef

1 onion, chopped

1 bell pepper, chopped

4 stalks celery, chopped

2 cloves garlic, crushed

1/3 c. catsup

3 T. water

20 saltine crackers. crushed

2 egg whites

1 t. pepper

1 t. basil

2 T. parsley flakes

1/2 t. hickory smoke salt

Combine all ingredients. Shape into patties. Freeze on a cookie sheet. When completely frozen, stack in a zipper plastic bag with pieces of waxed paper between patties. If you like catsup on top of your meatloaf, pack a zipper bag containing 2 c. additional catsup.

Rumpstrap

1 16 oz. can sliced peaches in juice

3 potatoes

Wash and dry potatoes, store in a net bag. Pack peaches.

Panniers Pecan Delight

1 c. caramels

1/2 c. raisins

1/2 c. chopped raisins

1/2 c. chopped pecans

3 c. crisp rice cereal

2 T. margarine

Take the wrapper off each caramel and bag. Store raisins, chopped pecans, and cereal together. Bag margarine separately.

In-the-field preparation

Fry patties in a covered skillet. Flip. Slice potatoes thin. Open peaches. Drain juice into the smaller pot. Add potatoes and about a cup of water. Cover and bring to a boil over medium heat. Stir frequently, adding more water if necessary to cook potatoes. When tender, add peaches. Top meatloaf with catsup and serve with potatoes. For dessert, melt 1 T. margarine in the large pot over medium heat. Add caramels, stirring constantly until melted. Throw in raisins and cereal. Stir until coated. Coat skillet with 1 T. margarine. Spread mixture into it and allow it to set up for five minutes. Cut into bite-sized pieces. Eat while still warm. If any is left over, heat slightly in the skillet before eating as the caramel will harden when cool.

THIS MEAL *needs no adaptation for float, car camping, or goat trips. For backpacking, dehydrate meat, vegetables, and peaches. Substitute 3 tomatoes (chopped and dried) for catsup, omit eggs (replace with additional water), and instead of making patties, cook it up in a large pot with enough water to make it like stew.*

After dinner, we move the picketed Boulderdash and Prancer, for as Miller wrote, "all [the grass] is eaten down pretty close by morning." Since Sandy has shown herself to be something of a troublemaker, Teri stakes the mule out for the night as well. The others we tie to a highline, a rope tied between two trees that acts like a hitching post for the horses.

DAY TWO MENU

Breakfast

Mexican Sombrero

Hot Chocolate

Trail Lunch

Cold Cuts with Chinese Hot Mustard

Peanut Butter and Chopped Prunes

Fresh Fruit

Dinner

Campfire Beans

Broccoli and Corn

Watermelon

DAY TWO

Being the cook, whether hired or volunteer, offers a great advantage on backcountry trips. Everybody loves the cook, provided the food tastes good! Even Miller discovered this. Beside a drawing entitled *Breakfast at Sunrise*, he recorded, "The sketch represents 'our mess' at the morning meal. Jean who is pouring out coffee, seems to our hungry eyes more graceful than Hebe disposing Nectar, although he is more shap[e]less than a log of wood." We express similar feelings as we watch Alex dishing up our breakfast of Mexican sombrero, except for the bit about the wood!

Day Two Breakfast Recipe

Mexican Sombrero

6 eggs

1 onion, chopped

1 7 oz. can Salsa Verde (or a tomato-based salsa for less heat)

2 c. swiss cheese, diced

8 whole wheat flour tortillas

1 T. margarine

> *Dice cheese and bag. Freeze tortillas, keeping frozen until ready to leave. (It keeps them fresher longer in the field.) Store eggs in a plastic container designed for carrying into the backcountry. It's better to pack onions in either a paper or mesh bag. Storing them for any length of time in plastic promotes rot. Bag margarine separately. Don't forget the salsa.*

In-the-field preparation

> *Melt margarine in a skillet. Chop the onion. Sauté in margarine while beating the eggs in a large bowl. Add eggs, salsa, and cheese to onions. Cover and cook over medium heat. Flip once cheese melts and eggs begin to brown. Remove tortillas from package and warm on top of the skillet lid as the eggs cook. When eggs are done, cut into six wedges and place on top of the tortillas. Serve with hot chocolate.*
>
> *THIS MEAL needs no adaptation for float, car camping, or goat trips. Since powdered eggs aren't an adequate substitute for fresh eggs, choose a suitable breakfast from the other types of trips if you don't want the added weight of carrying in the eggs.*

Horses can cover thirty to forty miles a day unless forced to pick their way through rough, rocky terrain or high mountain passes. On this test run, we content ourselves with meandering through the low country of the Bridger National Forest, traveling less than half that distance each day.

Onyx's smooth walking gate lulls me with perpetual motion. Settling in my saddle, I watch the forest slip by. Snowcapped mountains on the horizon come into

view every now and then between breaks in the pines. An occasional hawk screeches or scolding magpies vie with the muffled thud clump of hoofbeats in the dirt. Even Sandy plods along with the peaceful attitude of the place.

Our wanderings bring us to the Big Sandy River. It cuts through the landscape of pines and open grasslands, churning with the runoff from late-spring snows. As we let the animals wade in and drink their fill, I'm reminded of Miller's *Scene on Big Sandy River*. "The sketch may be said to represent a small slice of an Indian paradise," he declared, "Indian women, horses, a stream of water, shade trees, and the broad prairie to the right." Glancing over my shoulder at riders, mounts, and pack animals,

76

I see the tradition of what Miller drew and wrote about. One by one the horses lift their heads, their thirst satiated, as we continue across the river.

About an hour down the trail, we meet up with a couple of hikers leading a pack horse that hauls all their gear like prospectors during the gold rush days. Similar to goat packing, some outfitters rent horses to people who enjoy hiking but prefer not to carry a backpack. This also cuts down on the number of horses needed on an animal-assisted trip, lessening the environmental impact.

The hikers stop, stepping off the trail so when we pass by, our horses won't spook at any unexpected sight or movement. Blaze whinnies and Dancer snorts at these new-comers. Onyx nearly twists his head off, peering back at them in a sizing-up manner.

The afternoon grows warm. With the heat come the mosquitoes and the biting flies. Before long, the animals start to fidget. Knowing the restlessness will soon turn into irritability, Teri guides the pack string off the trail and into a shaded patch of pines. She dismounts, ties the animals to the trees, and then takes a plastic bottle with a trigger nozzle from her saddlebags as the rest of us follow suit.

Boulderdash lets Teri spray the pungent fly repellent on his coat without so much as a twitch of his skin. Sandy, on the other hand, acts like she's being doused with acid, shying away every time Teri comes near, stomping her hooves, trying to kick. Joy pulls a faded bandana from her pocket. She drenches it with fly spray while Teri and Kirk take up positions on each side of Sandy's head. The two hold the mule steady, murmuring in soothing tones as Joy wipes the cloth over Sandy's neck and legs. Easygoing Smoke also takes exception to the stuff and must be coaxed into standing still by Alex and me while Teri rubs him down.

In the 1800s, travelers didn't worry about biting insects on themselves, their animals, or even in the food. Bread recipes mentioned in *Oregon Trail* journals occasionally described how dough would turn black from swarms of mosquitoes getting stuck in it. Since cooks couldn't prevent this, they simply baked the bread, mosquitoes and all! That evening, when we select a campsite in one of the mountains' abundant meadows, we look forward to a bug-free dinner.

Day Two Dinner Recipes

Campfire Beans

2 15 1/2 oz. cans kidney beans   **1** t. nutmeg
1 lb. summer sausage   **1/4** c. sugar
1/4 c. powdered milk

    Mix milk, nutmeg, and sugar and bag together. Store beans and sausage separately.

Broccoli and Corn

1 16 oz. pkg. frozen broccoli   **1** 16 oz. pkg frozen corn

Dehydrate the vegetables and pack in a zipper plastic bug.

Watermelon

1 watermelon

Put the whole melon in a plastic bag just before leaving on the trip. (If stored too long in plastic, it will promote rot. But the plastic will protect other items in the pannier should the melon burst.)

In-the-field preparation

Rehydrate the broccoli and corn. Bring a pot of water to boil for cooking the vegetables and for hot drinks. Slice summer sausage and combine it with the other Campfire Beans ingredients in a skillet. When the broccoli and corn are reconstituted, add them to the boiling water and cook, covered, over medium heat until tender. Slice and serve the watermelon for dessert.

THIS MEAL needs no adaptation for car camping, goat, and float trips. For backpacking, substitute dehydrated beans and bulk sausage that has been browned before drying. Replace the watermelon with another lightweight dessert.

DAY THREE MENU

Breakfast

Whole Wheat Slam-Johns

Fresh Oranges

Trail Lunch

Deviled Ham and Chopped Dill
Pickles

Hot Carrot Spread

Fresh Fruit

Dinner

Salmon Manti

Mushroom Stuff

Fruit Cache

DAY THREE

Women on the *Oregon Trail* sometime referred to pancakes as "slam-johns." The *American Frugal Housewife*, published in 1833, instructed cooks to add flour until "the spoon moves round with difficulty. If they are thin, they are apt to soak fat. Have the fat in your skillet boiling hot, and drop them in with a spoon. . . . The more fat they are cooked in, the less they soak." Teri expertly flips our slam-johns this cloudy morning, creating stacks, which disappear as fast as they appear.

Day Three Breakfast Recipe

Whole Wheat Slam-Johns

1 c. whole wheat flour
2 T. powdered buttermilk
1/2 t. baking powder
1 t. salt

2 T. sugar
1/4 c. water
2 T. margarine

> *Mix and bag all ingredients except margarine.*

In-the-field preparation

> *While coffee water heats, mix 3/4 c. cold water with dry ingredients to make a batter. Melt some of the margarine in the skillet, enough to coat the bottom. Spoon batter into hot skillet. Cook, covered, over medium heat. Flip once after bottom browns and top gets firm, 2–4 minutes per side. If the outside is cooking too fast and inside is still raw, lower heat. Serve with honey or molasses and fresh oranges. Makes 12.*
>
> **THIS MEAL** *needs no adaptation to be suitable for all types of trips.*

Day Three Lunch Recipe

Hot Carrot Spread

1/4 head cabbage
3 carrots

1/2 c. raisins
hot English mustard

> *Store ingredients separately.*

In-the-field preparation

> *Shred cabbage and carrots. Mix in raisins and enough mustard to hold mixture together. Spread on bread, tortillas, rolls, or bagels.*
>
> **THIS LUNCH** *is suitable for car camping, goat, and float trips.*

Clouds boil like oatmeal in a big gray pot. A few sprinkles announce the forthcoming rain, forcing us to break camp in a hurry before everything gets wet. Once we get the horses saddled and the panniers loaded, the canvas mantis protect the contents from the now persistent cold drizzle. I don my cowboy hat and slicker, just two pieces of the quintessential and very fashionable cowboy apparel. But cowboy hats, boots, and slickers all have their roots planted in the practical. Good felt hats guard against the bright sunshine and shield your eyes from windblown sand or snow. The compressed felt also repels water, and the brim's wide shape acts like a gutter, keeping frigid rainwater from dripping down your face and the back of your neck. Pointed-toe construction of cowboy boots allow for quick access into the stirrup of a wheeling horse while the heel stops your foot from slipping through the stirrup and becoming caught.

Then there's the slicker. Especially designed for horseback use, the mustard-colored 1880s Pommel Slicker, also called a "fishskin" or "tower" saddle coat, was made of a heavy canvas or duct material that had been waterproofed with linseed oil. Other than utilizing modern rain-repellent fabric, today's slicker differs little from the original pattern. The long split up the back allows the ankle-length coat to cover the entire saddle as well as the rider, making for a nice dry ride on a wet day. So I maintain a dry seat even when it starts to pour in earnest.

Before long, we begin to look like extras in a Clint Eastwood Western. Rain streams from our hats each time we glance down. The horses hang their heads. Their coats darken and slick down with moisture. It beads on the canvas mantis and rolls off the sides in mini waterfalls. But our food remains dry.

Horse hooves squish in the mud as the deluge splatters against the ground. Each time one of the packs rubs against tree boughs, it releases the aromatic pine scent into the damp air. When the wind changes, blowing freezing rain down from the north, we stop and make camp in the first patch of grassland we come to.

Alonzo Delano, one of countless thousands of forty-niners struck with gold fever, faced a similar situation on his way to California, which he wrote about in *Life on the Plains and at the Diggings* (1854). After a stormy day where "it seemed as if a water spout was discharging its floods upon us," Delano went on to note, "Our stoves were put into our tents, and the covers of boxes, or stray pieces of wood in the wagons, were used to start a fire, and then buffalo chips were heaped upon the stoves until they got dry enough to burn, and in this way we contrived to do our cooking."

Delano finished the day's entry with "distance, nothing," which sums up our day as well. Teri sets up the two-burner stove in the vestibule of our tent. I turn the camp table on its side and place it so that it acts as a windshield against the blowing rain. Nevertheless, drops still fly in and land on the heating skillets of food and dance on the lids.

After we tend to the animals, everybody crowds into the tent, trying not to drip mud onto our meal as we squirm out of slickers and boots in the shelter of the vestibule and crawl inside. This kind of weather makes us wish for a wall tent which is about the size of a room in a small house. Instead we pass pans, ingredients, utensils, bowls, silverware, and finally food back and forth like an assembly line at an auto plant. But it makes the meal just that much more enjoyable because everybody participates in the preparation of our salmon feast.

Salmon was either dried, smoked, pickled, or packed in salt to preserve it until it became available canned to cooks by the 1840s. New England fishermen also packed fresh salmon in ice and shipped it via railroad to large cities such as New York and Philadelphia; however, it wasn't available to the Chicago area until 1851. So most people had to settle for canned. Immigrant workers cleaned, boned, and packed salmon in cans by hand until 1882 when a machine took over this labor-intensive job.

Day Three Dinner Recipes

Salmon Manti

2 14 3/4 oz. cans salmon
2 10 3/4 oz. cans cream of asparagus
  soup
1 onion
4 T. Worcestershire sauce

2 t. dry mustard
1 t. garlic powder
3 c. spinach noodles
1 T. margarine

Combine Worcestershire sauce, dry mustard, and garlic powder in a plastic bottle. Store onion in a net bag. Bag noodles and margarine separately. Pack cans of salmon and soup.

Mushroom Stuff

12 large mushrooms
1/2 bell pepper, chopped fine
1 1/2 slices bread

3 T. Parmesan cheese
1/4 c. margarine

Remove stems from mushrooms. Chop the stems. Dehydrate mushroom caps and stems, bell pepper, and bread. When dry, crumble bread and bag with pepper, stems, and cheese. Store mushroom caps and margarine in two separate bags.

Fruit Cache

2 16 oz. can fruit cocktail in juice   **1/3** c. raisins
1 11 oz. can Mandarin orange segments

Bag raisins. Pack cans of fruit

In-the-field preparation

Rehydrate mushroom caps and the bell pepper mixture. Open salmon. Pour fish and juice into an empty plastic bag. Add Worcestershire sauce mixture. Seal and gently squeeze until mixed. Set aside. Bring a large pot of water to boil. Add noodles. Cook uncovered until done, about 12 minutes. Stir occasionally. Meanwhile, melt 1/4 c. margarine in the skillet. Pour in pepper mixture and blend. Spoon mixture into caps. Arrange in the skillet and cook over low heat for 15 minutes. Chop onion. In smaller pot, melt 1 T. margarine and add onion. Stir over medium heat until tender. Add salmon mixture and soup. Cook until completely heated. Serve over drained noodles. For dessert, open cans of fruit. Add raisins. Serve.

THIS MEAL needs no adaptation for float, car camping, or goat trips. The Mushroom Stuff also needs no adaptation for backpacking. The Salmon Manti and Fruit Cache, however, is not suitable for backpacking unless you don't mind the extra weight of canned foods. Dried fruit mix can be substituted for Fruit Cache.

DAY FOUR MENU

Breakfast
Depuyer Biscuits
Timberline Gravy
Coffee

Trail Lunch
Sardine Sling
Parmesan Half Hitch
Fresh Fruit

Dinner
Horsepacker's Pie
A & P Barrel

DAY FOUR

"A cold wind blew this morning," wrote Delano the morning after the rain storm. "The sky was overcast with clouds, and the gloom and air of November, rather than the genial warmth of spring, hung over us." We wake to snow, which poses a completely different cooking problem for Kirk. All twigs are either buried in the snow or soaked from yesterday's rain. Rather than wasting fuel drying twigs in a pan on the stove, Kirk elects to make flip biscuits. Instead of forming half-inch rounds of dough (as called for in the recipe), he flattens each biscuit until it resembles a silver-dollar-sized pancake and places them in the skillet over a low heat. Halfway through the "baking" time, he turns them to cook both sides. Thus we have an adequate alternative to baked biscuits for our breakfast.

Indigenous peoples from the plains, whose primary food source came from the buffalo, found their own substitute for biscuits, called "depuyer" by the mountain men. Indigenous peoples took the ridge of fatty tissue that ran along the buffalo's backbone, dipped it in hot grease for half a minute, then hung it up inside the lodge to dry and smoke for twelve hours. Pieces of depuyer were cut from the main strap and served with fresh or dried meat.

Day Four Breakfast Recipes

Depuyer Biscuits

2 1/3 c. flour

1 t. salt

1 t. baking powder

1 t. baking soda

4 T. powdered buttermilk

3 1/2 T. margarine

Bag together all ingredients except margarine.

Timberline Gravy

1/2 lb. sausage

1/4 c. powdered milk

1 t. salt

2 1/2 T. flour

1 t. pepper

2 T. margarine

Brown sausage and dehydrate. Mix and bag powdered milk, salt, flour, and pepper. Bag sausage separately from margarine.

In-the-field preparation

Cut 3 1/2 T. margarine into biscuit mix. Add 3/4 c. cold water and squeeze to form soft dough. Pat into biscuits about 1/2-inch thick. Bake over low heat and lid fire for 10–12 minutes. Makes 14. When biscuits are done, keep warm in insulated bowls. Melt 2 T. margarine in skillet. Add sausage-and-powdered milk mixture. Stir constantly while adding 2 c. cold water. Bring to a boil, continuing to stir until gravy thickens. Serve over biscuits.

THIS MEAL *needs no adaptation for any type of trip.*

Day Four Lunch Recipes

Sardine Sling

2 3.75 oz. cans sardines in mustard
1 T. horseradish

1 T. reconstituted lemon juice
1 t. paprika

Mix horseradish, lemon juice, and paprika together and bag. Pack cans of sardines.

Parmesan Hitch

1 c. Parmesan cheese
1/2 t. cayenne

1 T. Worcestershire sauce
2 T. margarine

Mix cheese and cayenne and bag together. Store remaining ingredients separately.

In-the-field preparation

For Sardine Sling, mash all ingredients together in plastic bags. Spread on bread, bagels, or rolls. For Parmesan hitch, melt margarine; pour it and remaining ingredients in a plastic bag and mix by squeezing. Spread on bread, bagels, or rolls.

THIS LUNCH *is suitable for car camping, goat, and float trips.*

Horses stand with their backs to the storm, eyeing us warily as we break down camp. They paw through the accumulation to reach the meadow grass underneath. If we hadn't had to make do with a marginal pasture, we'd be tempted to just sit around the stove, drinking tea and telling stories, and wait out the storm. But the horses need better grazing.

Large flakes fall fast and wet, obstructing sight and sound. Wind whips through the trees, shaking clumps from the limbs in the same manner the animals employ to rid themselves of the blankets of white lining their backs. Hampered by the snowfall, it takes us longer than normal to round up the herd. Onyx stamps his feet at my approach, but he doesn't bound away like Blaze and Smoke do at Teri's advance. Hobbles only slow horses down. These quick-witted equines swiftly learn how to hop across a field with the agility of jackrabbits. But once captured, they settle down into the dependable animals we rely on in the wilderness.

The journals of enlisted men and officers alike who saw field service in the West tell of the hardships faced by the soldiers and their animals during the campaigns against the indigenous peoples in the post–Civil War years. Ill-equipped for the elements, these frontier regulars counted on their horses and mules for survival. When a snowstorm blew in, the men pulled their horses' feed bags over their (human) heads to protect their faces from the severe weather. Thus unable to see, the soldiers relied on the animals to find a way through the drifts to shelter. We, too, seek shelter as the snow thickens, cocooning us in white. Reining the horses off the trail, we bushwhack through the trees for a shorter path to a decent meadow where the animals can paw their way through the snow to graze. Here we set up camp.

Once we get the animals taken care of for the night, everybody helps Joy hunt for dead twigs lying at the bases of the trees. The snow prevents us from finding enough to bake our Horsepacker's Pie. So she boils the sliced potatoes, adding the rehydrated meat and peas, and cooks it until tender. Next she adds the canned mushroom soup. Meanwhile, she heats the tortillas in the skillet over low. Leaving one in the bottom, Joy pours the meat-and-vegetable mixture over it then tops the concoction with the other tortilla, not unlike what the pioneers did. When a scarcity of burnable fuel forced frontier cooks to improvise, meat-and-vegetable pies were boiled with either dumplings or bread crumbs as the crust, which they called the "paste."

Day Four Dinner Recipes

Horsepacker's Pie

2 potatoes
1 lb. ground beef
1 16 oz. pkg. frozen peas
1 10.5 oz. can cream of mushroom
   soup
2 large tortillas
1 T. parsley flakes

2 t. onion powder
1 t. garlic powder
1 t. pepper
2 T. soy sauce
2 T. Worcestershire sauce
1 T. margarine

Brown ground beef. Dehydrate meat and peas. Wash and pat dry potatoes before packing them in a net bag. Mix and bag together the parsley, onion powder, garlic powder, and pepper. Store soy sauce and Worcestershire sauce in plastic bottles. Pack margarine separately.

A & P Barrel

1 16 oz. can apricots in juice

1 20 oz. can pineapple chunks in juice

20 graham crackers

Pack each item separately.

In-the-field preparation

While water boils for hot drinks, rehydrate the meat and peas. Slice potatoes very thin. Melt margarine in the skillet. Place one tortilla in the bottom. Lay the potato slices on the tortilla. Add peas then ground meat. Sprinkle pepper mixture, soy, and Worcestershire sauces over meat and smear soup over the top. Lay the other tortilla on top. Cover. Bake over low heat and a lid fire for 30–35 minutes. For dessert, open apricots and pineapple. Mix together in a pot. Crush crackers over the top and serve.

*   **THIS MEAL** needs no adaptation for car camping, goat, or float trips. For backpacking, substitute dehydrated potatoes and leave out the soy sauce and Worcestershire sauce (unless you don't mind carrying the extra weight) and serve dried fruits for dessert.*

DAY FIVE MENU

Breakfast

Double Diamond Mincemeat

Coffee

Trail Lunch

Deviled Ham and Chopped Dill Pickles

Crab Pardner

Fresh fruit

Dinner

Mountain Meadow Eggplant

Shifty Eyed

End of the Rope

Tea

DAY FIVE

With snow continuing to fall at a furious rate. We opt for another "distance nothing" day and settled in for a cozy tent breakfast. The twigs we gathered yesterday have dried enough for a lid fire for our Double Diamond Mincemeat. In the sixteenth century, cooks preserved meat by making mincemeat. They chopped the meat (frequently tongue) very fine; added large quantities of spices such as mace, cloves, and nutmeg; sugar; chopped suet (fat); fruits such as raisins, currants, apples, lemons, and oranges; rosewater; and liquor (usually brandy or wine). This mixture was packed into crocks and salt sprinkled over the top. After covering the stone jars, cooks stored them in the root cellar.

Day Five Breakfast Recipe

Double Diamond Mincemeat

4 slices dried beef

1 c. mixed dried fruit

14 c. nuts, chopped

1 c. flour

1/4 c. brown sugar

1 t. baking powder

1 t. salt

2 T. powdered milk

4 T. margarine

Purchase thin-sliced dried beef in a jar. Bag it with fruit and nuts. Mix flour, sugar, baking powder, salt, and powdered milk and bag together. Store margarine separately.

In-the-field preparation

Bring beef mixture to a boil in 1 1/3 c. water in a covered pot. Boil for 2 minutes. Melt margarine in the skillet. Mix dry ingredients with 1 c. cold water to form a thick batter. Pour over melted margarine. Add fruit. Bake over low heat and a lid fire for 30 minutes, rotating for even cooking.

THIS MEAL needs no adaptation for any of the types of trips.

Day Five Lunch Recipe

Crab Pardner

1 6 oz. can crab meat

1 T. lemon juice

1 T. margarine

1/4 t. paprika

Pack each item separately.

In-the-field preparation

Mash all ingredients together in a plastic bag. Serve on bread, rolls, or tortillas.
THIS LUNCH *is suitable for goat, float, and car camping trips.*

During the fall and winter of 1823, trappers for the Ashley-Henry fur-trading company roamed through the Wind River Range. Originally, they had no plans to enter what would become Wyoming. Raids by Arikaras and Blackfeet along the Missouri River, however, persuaded the fur traders to redirect their operations to the central Rocky Mountains. After failing in an attempt to cross the region by means of Union Pass (near present-day Dubois), a party led by Jed Smith spent the spring of 1824 wandering down through another one hundred miles of the Winds (the local abbreviation for the range), searching for a pass through the south end of mountains the Crows had described.

Facing ground blizzards of wind-driven snow, the mountain men, which included such future elites in westward exploration as Jim Bridger, Bill Sublette, Jim Clyman, and Tom Fitzpatrick, ran low on food. Clyman and Sublette volunteered to travel down into the Wind River basin in search of game. At sundown, they sighted three buffalo in an open, exposed spot. Clyman wrote an account of this event in his journal, published in *Journal of a Mountain Man*. In it, he recalled their "horses being too poor to run"; they dismounted and approached the animals by "crawling over the ice and snow." Alerted to the human presence, the bison started to scatter. Clyman managed to get off a shot, wounding one in the shoulder. He trudged through the snow, tracking the animal while Sublette returned to get the horses they left over a mile back. At the edge of a "steep gutter," Clyman came upon the wounded buffalo and fired again, killing it. Unfortunately, when it keeled over, it fell into the ravine.

The sun had all but set by the time Sublette arrived with horses in tow. Of necessity, the men began the butchering process, cutting off a big slab of meat to cook over a sagebrush fire. Right before they finished eating, the "north wind arose and grew stronger and stronger and a cold frosty snow commenced falling." It scattered the fire and made for a sleepless night on the frozen ground.

Carrie Strahorn, who traversed the West by stagecoach from 1877 to 1907, called sagebrush the friend that saved people from Jack Frost. The leaves, which stay on the bush year-round, contain a good percentage of oil which burns fast and hot. Had Clyman and Sublette managed to keep their fire alight, they wouldn't have spent such a miserable night with only two blankets between them and the frozen ground.

By the next morning, the temperature had dipped to a dangerous level. The air instantly numbed anything exposed to it. Neither Sublette nor Clyman could force their fingers to work well enough to strike flint against steel in order to spark a fire in a scant pile of the sagebrush Clyman scraped together. In frustration, they resorted to shooting the brush with their rifles. Still no luck. Finally, Clyman ran his hand through the ashes from the previous evening's fire, discovering a live coal no "larger than a grain of corn." It proved enough to coax a flame out of the greasy, pungent leaves even though the wind continuously snatched away most of the branches the men fed to the fire.

Once they warmed up, Clyman and Sublette packed the meat on the horses and headed for the shelter of timber in the mountains. But they weren't out of danger yet. About four miles still to go, Clyman realized he was "liable to freeze" if he stayed on horseback. Dismounting, he led the team on foot, finding an old indigenous lodge once they "struck a grove of timber." Its one side still standing offered scant but practical shelter. Clyman set to work getting a fire going and hot food into

his companion who had fallen into a stupor caused by severe hypothermia. This incident took place in winter; however, it's been known to snow every month of the year in Wyoming.

Day Five Dinner Recipes

Mountain Meadow Eggplant

2 eggplants, sliced thin

Marinade for eggplant

2/3 c. mayonnaise

4 T. vinegar

2 T. lemon juice

2 t. salt

2 t. pepper

2 t. Worcestershire sauce

1 t. Tabasco

Blend together marinade items. Soak eggplant in marinate for 24 hours. Pat dry before drying.

Shifty Eyed

1 pkg. frozen peas and carrots

1 pkg. white sauce mix

Dehydrate peas and carrots. Do not thaw first. Bag separately from the sauce mix.

End of the Rope

1/2 lb. cheese

1 T. margarine

pretzels

In-the-field preparation

Reconstitute eggplant, peas, and carrots. After making hot drinks, pour 1 1/2 c. boiling water in saucepan and add peas and carrots. Cover. Bring to boil over high heat. Remove from stove. Place eggplant and 1 c. of cold water in the skillet. Cook over medium heat until tender, adding more water as needed. double-decker peas and carrots on top of eggplant (unless you have a two-burner stove). When ready for dessert, slice cheese thin and melt in margarine in a pot over low heat. Dip in pretzels.

THIS MEAL need no adaptation for any of the types of trips.

DAY SIX MENU

Breakfast

Molasses Mix

Coffee

Trail Lunch

Hard Salami with Sliced Cheddar and Horseradish

Peanut Butter with Banana Chips

Fresh Fruit

Dinner

Rope Jerker

Camp Custard

Tea

DAY SIX

Day Six Breakfast Recipe

Molasses Mix

1 c. flour

1 1/2 c. buckwheat flour

1 t. baking powder

1 t. baking soda

1 t. salt

3 T. powdered buttermilk

1/2 t. allspice

1 c. brown sugar, firmly packed

1/2 c. raisins

1 egg

1/2 c. molasses

1/4 c. margarine

Mix and bag together first nine ingredients. Store egg in carton. Bag margarine separately. Put molasses in plastic bottle.

In-the-field preparation

After coffee water heats, melt margarine in skillet. Pour in molasses, and 1 1/2 c. water into bag of flour mixture. Add egg. Reseal and squeeze gently to mix. Pour the thick batter into skillet. Cover and bake over low with a lid fire for 45–60 minutes.

THIS MEAL needs no adaptation for float, car camping, or goat trips. For backpacking, replace egg with extra water. (Cake will be heavier and less moist.)

From looking at this morning's sky, you'd never guess we'd had three full days of bad weather. Sunny, clear blue as far as the eye can see, and warm. Except under the dense forest, the snow melts away like a ghostly reminder. Although sloppy, it proves an easy walkout day for the horses. This morning, Teri decides to break up the pack string, and we swop off, leading Sandy, Blaze, and Smoke separately. The trio behaves well on individually lead ropes, following behind our mounts. Better than when strung together.

A few hours along the trail, we come upon a group of backpackers with a couple of dogs. Knowing that our horses might frighten easily, the hikers moved off the downhill side of the trail and told their dogs to be quiet while we pass. As I draw near, one of the dogs starts to whine and shake. Onyx dances into a sidestep. I murmur reassuringly in his ear while the dog's owner restrains it. When Sandy, who is right behind me, reaches the dog, she snorts and kicks up her heels but doesn't cause a scene or a rodeo. Thank goodness!

By late afternoon, we arrive at the road head and our waiting trailers. The horses and Sandy receive a big bucket of grain while we unload the panniers and stow the tack for the trip home. The animals seem reluctant to enter the trailers in preparation for leaving. For that matter, so do we, for as Reverend Stephen Riggs wrote in 1880, after he and his wife spent forty years in the West, "It has been marvelous in our eyes."

Day Six Dinner Recipes

Rope Jerker

1 lb. sausage
2 apples, sliced thin
1 onion, chopped
4 stalks celery, chopped
1/2 t. cinnamon

1/4 t cayenne
1 t. caraway seed
2 c. spinach noodles
1 T. cornstarch

Brown sausage. Dehydrate meat, apples, onion, and celery. Bag these with cinnamon, cayenne, and caraway seed. Bag cornstarch and noodles in two separate bags.

Camp Custard

1 2.9 oz. box custard mix
1/4 c. powdered milk

1 egg

Bag custard mix and powdered milk together. Store egg in carton.

In-the-field preparation

Rehydrate sausage, apples, onion, and celery. Make hot drinks. Add 1 c. water to sausage mixture and bring to boil over medium heat in a covered pot. Cook until tender. Meanwhile, collect small bowls. Blend custard mixture, egg, and 2 c. water. Heat over medium until it boils. Remove from heat. Pour into bowls and set aside. When sausage mixture is tender. Bring liquid level up to two cups again and return to a boil. Add noodles. Cook over medium heat until done, about 15 minutes. In 1/3 c. water add cornstarch, mix well. Stir into sausage mixture. Boil 1 minute. Serve.

THIS MEAL needs no adaptation for car camping, float, and goat trip. For backpacking, make custard without egg.

DAY SEVEN MENU

BREAKFAST
Bellmeal

Coffee

Trail Lunch
Corned Beef Hash and Horseradish

Dates Chopped with Almonds

Fresh Fruit

Dinner
Sawbucks

Horseshoes

DAY SEVEN

Day Seven Breakfast Recipe

Bellmeal

1/2 c. oats
1 t. salt

1/4 cantaloupe

> *Dehydrate cantaloupe. Bag separately from oats and salt.*

In-the-field preparation

> *Bring 1 1/4 c. cold water and cantaloupe chips to boil in a covered pot over high heat. Add oatmeal and cook 2 minutes.*
>> **THIS MEAL** *needs no adaptation for any type of trip.*

Day Seven Trail Lunch Recipe

Trail lunch

1 15 oz. can corned beef hash
horseradish to taste
rolls

2 8 oz. box pitted dates
2 2 oz. pkg. almond slivers
fresh fruit

> *Pack canned corned beef hash and the rolls separately. Mix dates and almonds together. Divide by the number of people on the trip and bag individual portions.*

In-the-field preparation

> *Spread corned beef hash and horseradish to taste and distribute to participants with date-and-almond mix and fresh fruit of choice for storage in their individual saddle bags.*
>> **THIS MEAL** *needs no adaptation for goat, float, or car camping trips.*

Day Seven Dinner Recipes

Sawbucks

1 10 oz. pkg. frozen corn
5 chicken franks, sliced thin
6 tomatoes, chopped
1 onion, chopped

1 bell pepper, chopped
4 c. egg noodles
1/4 t. cayenne pepper
1 t. chili powder

Dehydrate corn, franks, tomatoes, onion, and bell pepper. Do not thaw corn first. When dry, bag with pepper and chili powder. Store noodles separately.

Horseshoes

12 T. chunky peanut butter   **3** T. sugar
1 T. cocoa

Mix cocoa and sugar and bag. Purchase a small plastic jar of peanut butter for the field.

In-the-field preparation

Rehydrate meat and vegetables. In a large, covered pot, bring meat and vegetables to boil in an additional 2 c. of cold water. When food is tender, add more water to bring level up to 2 1/2 c. When it is boiling again, add noodles. Cook over medium heat until done, about 15 minutes.

Drop peanut butter by teaspoons into cocoa sugar mix one at a time. Roll around until the outside is coated. Pop them into your mouth. (Kids love to make these!)

THIS MEAL *needs no adaptation for any type of trip.*

CHAPTER THREE

FIVE DAYS IN THE RED DESERT
TREKKING WITH GOATS

Harnessed to carts, goats have hauled necessities, luxuries, and humans for centuries. Yet utilizing them as true pack animals in the ways traditional to horses and mules only came about three decades ago. Since then, goat packing has thrived as an alternative for people who love to trek through the backcountry but don't enjoy carrying the heavy weight of backpacks.

Outfitted goat packing excursions generally last from three to five days. While some full-service (hired cook) trips exist, usually everybody does their own cooking. Following this rule of thumb, here are five days' worth of menus and meals suitable for this type of animal-assisted trek.

FOOD FOR THE TRAIL

Since you'll be hiking alongside the goats and you'll carry trail food in your day pack, choose from the lunches listed below or from the lists given in the backpacking or horse packing sections. Keep in mind your exertion level will be lower than when you backpack, therefore plan for approximately 1/3 pound of trail food per person per day.

It's only fair to warn you. You may have to fend off a few goats over delectables such as peanut butter and jelly sandwiches, bagels, muffins, tortillas, and fresh fruit. After all, goats are just big kids who love PB and J sandwiches and crisp apples as much as we humans do. I usually choose from the following:

- peanut butter and jelly sandwiches
- bagels filled with chopped chutney
- refried beans (canned) spread on tortillas
- summer sausage and rolls
- assorted fresh fruit
- tuna (canned) mixed with ketchup on English muffins
- muffins
- assorted hard candies

- shrimp (canned) with powdered onion and mustard on rye crackers
- chocolate-covered graham crackers
- molasses cookies
- oatmeal cookies

Supply list (5 days)

Baking Staples

1 10 oz. container baking powder
1 16 oz. box baking soda
1 lb. blue cornmeal (can substitute yellow)
1 lb. brown sugar
1 8 oz. container cocoa
1 lb. box cornstarch
1 5 lb. sack white flour

1 5 lb. sack whole wheat flour
1 5 lb. sack sugar
1 lb. jar honey
1 bottle of vanilla extract
1 18 oz. container oats
1 lb. can powdered buttermilk
1 25.6 oz box powdered milk
1 26 oz. box salt

Bread Products

1 pkg. English muffins

1 pkg. tortillas

Canned Goods

2 15 oz. can corned beef hash
1 2.25 oz. can sliced black olives

1 4 oz. can chopped green chilies
1 16 oz. sliced peaches in juice

Dried Fruit/Vegetables/Nuts

1 2 oz. pkg. almond slivers

1 container candied fruits

Fresh Fruit

1 cantaloupe
7 tomatoes

1 honeydew melon

Fresh Vegetables

1 bell pepper
1 head cabbage
1 1 lb. bag carrots
1 bunch celery

1 eggplant
7 onions
1 Bermuda onion
2 yellow squash

Frozen Food

1 16 oz. pkg. frozen blueberries

1 10 oz. pkg. frozen green beans

Meat/Milk/Margarine/Cheese/Eggs

2 lb. ground beef

1 1/2 lb. ground sausage

1 1/2 lb. ground turkey

1 lb. ham

1 lb. beef

1/4 lb. cheddar cheese

1 8 oz. container Parmesan cheese

6 eggs

1 1/2 lb. margarine (optional canned milk, see recipes below)

Rice/Noodles

1 16 oz. pkg. spinach noodles

1 16 oz. pkg. macaroni

Sauce & Other Mixes/Drinks/Specialty Items

1 6 oz. box cornmeal stuffing mix

2 1.6 oz. pkg. Hollandaise Sauce Mix

1 4 oz. pkg. ranch dressing mix

1 16 oz. box instant mashed potatoes

1 box rennet

1 lb. coffee

40 bags of assorted teas

1 10 oz. pkg. regular marshmallows

Spices

1 container allspice

1 container caraway seeds

1 container cayenne pepper

1 container cinnamon

1 container ground coriander seed

1 container cumin

1 container garlic powder

1 container ginger

1 container mace

1 container nutmeg

1 container parsley flakes

1 container pepper

1 bottle vanilla

TRAIL LUNCHES

1/3 lb. per person per day (see list above)

EXTRAS FOR THE TRAIL:

A plastic bottle of soy sauce, Worcestershire sauce, honey, molasses, salt, and pepper.

DAY ONE MENU

Breakfast

High Plains Hash

Coffee

Trail Lunch

Rye Crackers

Fresh Fruit

Oatmeal Cookies

Dinner

Tortillas des Carnes

Ensalada de Col

Melon

Tea

DAY ONE

No trails exist in much of Wyoming's two and a half million acres high plains Red Desert, other than those made by wild horses and pronghorns. Dry creek beds abound. Scattered bone fragments tell tales of hardship. And rising five hundred feet out of this strange-looking land of sage and sand, the Honeycombs Buttes look carved by time's knife, exposing every color from deep magenta to olive green.

The March morning dawns with a mass of gun-metal gray clouds. John, our guide, keeps an eye on them as he fixes a broken strap on one of the pack saddles. Jeff stows gear in a set of panniers, the term for saddlebags used on pack animals. But I alone capture the attention of our seven curious pack goats because I'm fixing breakfast, High Plains Hash.

Back in the 1600s, "hash" described a wide variety of dishes made from left-over meat and vegetables. Settlers chopped the ingredients very fine, put them into a kettle of boiling water, added a bit of salt and pepper, and sprinkled enough dry flour over the mixture to produce a thick gravy. In the US Army of the 1700s and 1800s, the only difference between hash, stew, and soup was the amount of water used. One cook in 1866 claimed four quarts of beans, two pounds of hash "boiled to rags in fifty quarts of water, will furnish a good meal for forty men" for about two cents per serving.

Day One Breakfast Recipe

High Plains Hash

6 eggs **6** English muffins

2 15 oz. can corned beef hash **2** 1.6 oz pkg. Hollandaise Sauce Mix

Wrap toilet paper around each egg and re-place it in the carton. Tie the container closed. Pack remaining ingredients separately. Place eggs in the top of the pannier.

In-the-field preparation

After making coffee, place a large pot on the stove filled with cold water. Add eggs. Cover and bring to boil over high heat. Remove from stove and set aside. Open hash. Heat in saucepan. Meanwhile, collect large bowls. Place half of a muffin in the bottom of each bowl. When hash is heated, spoon 1/8 of it into each bowl. Repeat with another two alternating layers of muffin and hash. Put lids on bowls to keep food warm while preparing sauce. Blend 2 c. of cold water and the sauce mix. Heat over medium heat, stirring constantly until sauce thickens. Peel hard-boiled eggs, reserving water for a round of hot drinks or washing up. Slice eggs. Arrange over the top layer of hash and muffins. Pour sauce over eggs and serve.

THIS MEAL requires no adaptation for use on horse packing, car camping, or float trips. It is only suitable on a backpack trip if you don't mind some extra weight caused by carrying canned hash and fresh eggs in a special plastic egg container (powdered eggs don't make an adequate substitute as they don't taste very good). As an option, the hash can be dehydrated. Allow for reconstituting time.

When it rains in the desert, the landscape turns to slick mud, almost impossible to trek through. Fortunately, the clouds dissipate by the time we pack up and head into what the locals simply call the "Honeycombs."

Since Jeff and I have asked John to show us the benefits of packing with goats, he immediately leads us up an almost perpendicular column of fifty-million-year-old claystone that crumbles even as our fingers clutch for handholds. The goats dash past us like children playing tag on a level field. And they carry seventy pounds in their scaled-down pack saddles John designed and produces himself. Resembling a sawbuck used on horses, John has modified the goat saddle so that it rides just behind the animal's shoulder blades and stops short of the hipbone. A rumpstrap and breast collar help keep saddle and cargo securely in place whether the goats amble straight up a column of claystone or trot down a steep gully.

The entire rig can be removed from a goat's back in a couple of minutes. As a demonstration, John stops next to Alpie, our lead goat and veteran of many pack trips. John removes the two five-gallon jugs of water from Alpie's panniers, unbuckles the cinch and two straps, then lifts saddle and blankets while the goat walks out from under it.

Jeff and I get in some practice by transferring the payload to Bob, a tenacious two-year-old. Still a teenager in goat years, Bob shouldn't haul this kind of weight for more than a few hours. When he begins to tire, we switch the water onto Menu's back. Menu received that name because he was scheduled to be on the menu at a goat breeders' conference until his owner attended a lecture John gave on goat packing and thought Menu had the right temperament for it. Menu reminds me of a family dog, lying down next to me when we stop for lunch on the sandy shore of an evaporated creek bed. I lean back against one of his panniers, using the brim of my hat to shade my eyes from the sun's relentless glare. He sighs and stretches his front legs out before him, half-dozing in the afternoon heat. His head sways slightly from side to side as the three of us talk. But the minute I rattle a plastic bag containing oatmeal cookies, he snaps his head around, cranes his neck forward, his lips begging for a morsel. Definitely reminiscent of "man's best friend."

After Menu receives his treat, I fix our lunch. Opening the can of tiny shrimp, I dump the contents into a plastic bag containing a bit of onion powder and mustard. Resealing the bag, I squeeze the contents until they are well mixed. Then I peel back the top so everybody can get to the filling to spread it on the rye crackers, not their hands.

Like us, goats can put in an eight- to ten-mile day in rough country. In the plains of the Red Desert, they can trek fifteen to twenty miles per day. Because goats can't sweat to keep cool, John refrains from traveling during the hottest part of the day or journeys by moonlight on summer desert trips. Fortunately for all of us, the constant breeze holds the sun's heat at bay on this springtime excursion.

When dusk approaches, we descend into a depression in the side of one of the buttes to get out of the ever-present wind. Following rule number one when out with pack animals, we tend to them first. After we strip off the panniers and saddles, we stack the tack and place the blankets out to dry in what's left of the sunshine. Next Jeff and I get to experience the most unique part of packing with goats, milking our doe Bonita. She provides us with a supply of fresh milk for drinking, cooking, and cheese on the journey.

John then hands us some alfalfa pellets, and all the goats gather around. Long-necked Sweet Pea captures more than his fair share. In all the jostling, many of the cubes land on the ground. Not to worry. Unlike grain that scatters rather than gets consumed, Newlio steps in and gobbles them right up, leaving nothing behind. Later the goats disburse around the campsite and munch on some greasewood. Of all the pack animals available today (including llamas), goats impact fragile environments the least. Instead of mowing native grasses, they nibble a bit of sagebrush here, crunch a few pine needles or willows there, or nip at some bitterbrush. Just like people, mealtime variety makes goats happy campers.

Then it's time to light the stove and begin preparing our dinner, Tortillas des Carnes. Mexican foods go great with hot weather. By the end of the Mexican War in 1848, south-of-the-border cuisine had become a popular and a welcome addition to the American diet. Meat was generally prepared with the liberal amounts of either red or green chilies that had been blistered and peeled before mixing them with the meat. Cooks accomplished this by holding the peppers one at a time over the flames of an open fire pit until the pepper's skin charred and bubbled. Once brown, the peppers were placed, still hot, in a covered jar and allowed to sweat until they cooled enough to handle. This made it easier to peel off the skins. Finally the chilies were ready to use.

Day One Dinner Recipes

Tortillas des Carnes

1 lb. beef, sliced
8 tortillas
1 onion
1 2.25 oz. can sliced black olives

1 4 oz. can chopped green chilies
1 t. cumin
1 T. margarine

Sprinkle cumin on beef slices. Freeze in a zipper bag. Also freeze tortillas. Pack re-maining ingredients for trip, storing onion in a net bag and keeping margarine separate. When ready to leave on the trip, bag both frozen items together and keep in an ice chest until packing them in the panniers.

Ensalada de Col

1/3 head of cabbage

1 small Bermuda onion

1 bell pepper

1 4 oz. pkg. ranch dressing mix

4 T. powdered buttermilk

1/2 c. goat milk

Place the cabbage section and bell pepper in a vegetable zipper bag. Store onion in the net bag. Mix and bag together dressing mix and buttermilk powder. The goat milk will be obtained in the field. If no producing doe is scheduled for your trip, substitute 1/4 c. powdered milk and blend with dressing mixture before bagging. Keep fresh vegetables in an ice chest until ready to pack in the panniers at the road head.

Melon

1 honeydew melon

Pack whole for the trip.

In-the-field preparation

Melt margarine in the skillet. Chop onion. Stir-fry meat and onion in the margarine over medium heat until cooked. Lay tortillas on the lid while meat cooks in order to heat them. Open olives and green chilies, draining each. Add them to the meat mixture, stirring until well mixed. Cover and remove from heat. Collect large bowls and put on a pot of water for tea and doing dishes. Shred cabbage and place in large pot. Chop bell pepper and onion. Add goat milk to bag of dressing mixture. Reseal and gently squeeze until blended. Pour over cabbage. Mix well. Serve in bowls. Serve meat mixture rolled up in warm tortillas. Slice melon and serve. Give pepper and melon seeds and rind to the goats.

THIS MEAL requires no adaptation for horse packing, car camping, or float trips. For backpacking, dehydrate meat, onion, and canned vegetables used in the Tortillas des Carnes and the fresh vegetables used in the Ensalada de Col. Substitute 4 T. powdered milk and 1/2 c. water for the fresh in accordance with the recipe. Fresh honeydew can be carried if you don't mind the extra weight. Otherwise, select a lighter backpacking dessert as the flavor washes out of honeydew when it's been dried then reconstituted.

Once we finish dinner, John extracts a button squeeze box, a small accordion-like instrument, from one of the panniers and plays a polka. The goats cluster around us, listening and falling asleep one by one as the polka drifts into a waltz. Unlike horses, goats don't require fencing, hobbling, or highline tying to keep them near camp overnight. They enjoy people's company. In fact, Menu beds down in the vestibule of our tent, staying there through much of the night.

DAY TWO MENU

Breakfast

Cantaloupe Crepes
Coffee

Trail Lunch

Peanut Butter and Jelly Sandwiches
Chocolate Covered Graham Crackers
Fresh Fruit

Dinner

Army Life Stew
Whole Wheat Biscuits
Mexican Cheese Pudding
Tea

DAY TWO

Next morning, we breakfast on Cantaloupe Crepes. A member of the muskmelon family, this fruit has been cultivated in America since colonial days. People ate it raw, sliced, or combined with other in-season fruits for breakfast or with ice cream for dessert. However, industrious jelly makers turned the melon into cantaloupe conserve, a type of jam, and served it with bread.

Day Two Breakfast Recipe

Cantaloupe Crepes

1 cantaloupe
1 c. flour
1/4 c. sugar
1/2 t. salt
1/4 t. coriander

5 T. margarine
1/4 c. sugar
1 t. cinnamon
1/4 t. mace
goat milk

Pack cantaloupe whole for the trip. Mix next four ingredients together and bag. Mix sugar and spices together and store in separate bag from the margarine. If no milking doe will accompany you, substitute 1/4 c. powdered milk for the fresh and bag it in with flour mixture.

In-the-field preparation

Chop cantaloupe, giving seeds and rind to the goats while the water is boiling for coffee. Add 1 c. of water to flour mixture, making a thin batter. Melt a bit of margarine in the skillet to lightly grease it. Spoon about 2 T. of batter into the skillet, tilting it to spread batter. Flip when crepe browns on the bottom and bubbles on top, cooking the other side. Repeat until all batter is used. Sprinkle cinnamon sugar mix over the top of each crepe. Spoon on some cantaloupe and serve. Makes 7–8 crepes.

THIS MEAL needs no adaptation on car camping, horse packing, and float trips. For backpacking, dehydrate the melon then reconstitute it when ready to fix breakfast.

When we break camp, we inspect the site for telltale signs of our presence. There are none. Goats tread virtually unnoticed in the wilderness because the tracks and droppings they leave behind blend in with those of deer, pronghorn, or bighorn sheep.

Normally, one goat hauls all supplies for one person. We brought more in order to cache water for John's summer excursions into the desert. Plus, two rookies came along, sporting extra light loads so they could "learn the ropes." Like their human counterparts, kids master packing by watching the grown-ups. Actual training begins as early as two weeks to a month old. John brings the youngsters along with mom as soon as they are able to keep up with the herd; this way they accept traveling in rainy weather and getting their feet wet, literally. Goats tend to shy away from water and leap over streams whenever possible. But when the kids (the goat kind) see the adults crossing wider creeks without complaint, they follow suit.

As the kids grow, John introduces them to pack saddles by fashioning a cinch strap from a soft belt covered with thick layers of burlap. He wraps it around the kid's middle. Once they accept it, John attaches a blanket to the strap. By the time they reach five or six months, they wear a mini version of a saddle with short panniers. At a year old, bucks can pack about thirty pounds. An adult wether (neutered buck) can carry close to one-third of his body weight, or about seventy to seventy-five pounds. Does can haul between twenty-five and thirty pounds. Of course, they also furnish milk! Once we make camp and milk Bonita, I begin dinner. The Whole Wheat Biscuits require baking; however, in the desert, twigs can be a rare commodity. So instead of using a lid fire, I pat the biscuits quite flat and cook them like pancakes over the stove's lowest heat, flipping them to "bake" one side at a time. Then I fix the Army Life Stew.

While beef never replaced pork as the main meat rationed to American soldiers during the eighteenth and nineteenth centuries, when supplies were available, each enlisted man received one and one-quarter pound of either fresh or salt beef per day. And the army regulated how the meat could be cooked! The beef was cubed and simmered in a pot of water for precisely one and one-half hours. Any vegetables in season (many forts had gardens to supplement vegetable rations, which usually consisted of beans or peas), potatoes, if available, and salt were added. The brew was simmered about two hours until the meat became tender.

Day Two Dinner Recipes

Army Life Stew

1 lb. ground beef
1/2 lb. ground turkey
6 carrots
6 stalks celery
2 onions

2 c. macaroni
2 T. parsley flakes
1 t. nutmeg
1 t. cayenne
1/2 c. Parmesan cheese

Brown beef and turkey together. Freeze in a zipper bag with parsley, nutmeg, pepper, and cheese. Wash and dry carrots and celery. Store in vegetable zipper bag. Put onion in net bag. Bag macaroni separately. (If you will be traveling in a hot climate, dehydrate the beef and turkey after browning.)

Whole Wheat Biscuits

1 2/3 c. whole wheat flour
1/3 c. flour
4 T. powdered buttermilk
1 t. salt

1 t. baking powder
1 t. baking soda
3 T. margarine

Blend and bag all ingredients except margarine.

Goat Milk Custard

3 c. goat milk
4 T. sugar
2 T. vanilla
1 1/2 tablets rennet

1/3 c. honey
1 t. coriander
1 t. allspice

Mix honey with coriander and allspice. Store in a small plastic bottle. Also store va-nilla in plastic bottle. Bag sugar and rennet tablets separately. Goat milk will be obtained in the field. If you are not packing with a producing doe, substitute 1/2 c. powdered milk and 3 c. water. NOTE: canned milk cannot be substituted for fresh or powdered as it won't react to the rennet well enough to create a firm custard.

In-the-field preparation

Chop carrots, celery, and onion. Place all stew ingredients in the large pot. Cover and bring to a boil over high heat in enough water to cover mixture. Boil for 5 minutes then remove from heat and wrap in a piece of Ensolite to keep stew warm. Collect large and small bowls.

While water for tea is heating, cut margarine into biscuit mix. Add 1 1/4 c. of cold water to dry ingredients or enough to form a soft dough. Pat into biscuits about 1/2 inch thick. Bake in the skillet with a lid fire 10–12 minutes until browned. Makes 12–14. Re-turn stew to the stove and simmer 15–20 minutes or until vegetables are tender. Serve with biscuits.

When ready for dessert, combine milk, sugar, and vanilla in smaller pot. Heat over low fire until lukewarm (just barely warm to the touch when you dip your finger in milk). Meanwhile, dissolve rennet in 2 T. cold water. When milk is warm, add rennet, stirring vigorously for three seconds only. Pour mixture into bowls and set aside. Leave undistrib-uted for 15 minutes. Heat honey and spices in smaller pot (don't need to clean out first) until warm. Pour over pudding and serve.

THIS MEAL *needs no adaptations for horse packing, car camping, or float trips. For backpacking, dehydrate all the meat and vegetables in the stew recipe. Substitute powdered milk for fresh in the custard.*

DAY THREE MENU

Breakfast

Blue Cornmeal Mush
Coffee

Trail Lunch

Bagels with Chopped Chutney
Fresh Fruit
Assorted Hard Candies

Dinner

Eggplant Bonita
Desert Blueberry Pie
Tea

DAY THREE

For breakfast, I prepare Blue Cornmeal Mush. Blue corn, indigenous to New Mexico, adds an earthy flavor to the traditional version of what settlers called "stirabout," "porridge," and even "hasty pudding." Pilgrims learned how to fix this simple dish from the indigenous peoples. They threw handfuls of cornmeal into a pot of boiling water, added a bit of salt, and cooked it about half an hour, stirring constantly to keep lumps from forming. One frontier cook claimed mush and johnnycake (cornbread) were all human beings needed to start the day.

Day Three Breakfast Recipe

Blue Cornmeal Mush

1 1/4 c. blue cornmeal   **3** T. sugar
1 t. salt   **3** T. powdered milk

      Mix all ingredients and bag.

In-the-field preparation

After heating water for coffee, stir cornmeal mix into 4 c. cold water that has been poured into the large pot. Cover. Bring to boil over medium heat. Reduce to low and cook 5 minutes, stirring constantly

THIS MEAL *requires no adaptation for any of the other trips.*

We stop at an anthill about a foot in diameter. Ever the curious one, Julio sniffs it. John scoops a handful of sand and rock chips the ants have mounded, letting it trickle through his fingers as he checks for flakes. Flakes refer to micro slivers broken off of stones as indigenous peoples fashioned them into tools or arrowheads. Lots of flakes on an anthill suggests an indigenous camping ground some place in the vicinity. Archaeologists have discovered pit houses dating back 6,500 years in the Red Desert. The indigenous hunter-gatherer cultures flourished in what looks like absolute desolation to the untrained eye. They harvested the ricegrass we walk through and the biscuit root. Plains Nations actually used the latter as trail food. Besides eating the roots raw (they taste like a cross between a sweet potato and a turnip), the indigenous peoples dried the roots and ground them into flour. Afterward, they baked the bread, known as *cous*, in the shape of a doughnut, strung them through a thong of leather and hung them from the horse, the equivalent of trail bagels. Our bagels aren't so exotic, but we find them just as tasty, spreading fruity chutney on the halves for a satisfying lunch.

Caverns, like those John caches water in, abound in the Honeycombs. We take full advantage of one when lightning hits nearby. It's close enough that it buzzed in Jeff's ears, so we scramble into the cave and wait for the storm to pass. Inside we find a stash of driftwood caught and held among the mudstone formation. This means I can bake a blueberry pie tonight instead of having to convert the recipe into blueberry pancakes.

Early colonists found many berries that looked familiar to them, especially blueberries. However, they mistook them for the English bilberry. Cooks preserved berries by boiling them in some sugar until the ingredients turned into a thick syrup. Then they spread the fruit on pieces of paper and laid them in the sun to dry. Once dehydrated, these forerunners to what we call "fruit leather" were rolled up and stored in a dry place. When the family wanted blueberry pie, the cook pealed off enough berry filling from the paper and dropped it in a pan of boiling water and sugar until reconstituted.

Day Three Dinner Recipes

Eggplant Bonita

1/2 lb. sausage	**4** stalks celery, chopped
1 eggplant, chopped	**1/3** c. margarine
4 tomatoes, chopped	**1** 6 oz. box cornmeal stuffing mix
1 onion, diced	

Brown sausage before dehydrating. Dehydrate eggplant, tomatoes, onion, and celery. Bag sausage and onion together (or onion can be taken fresh into the field). Bag remaining vegetables with the seasoning packet that comes with the stuffing mix. Store stuffing bread and margarine separately.

Desert Blueberry Pie

1 1.6 oz. pkg. frozen blueberries	**1** T. cornstarch
1/2 c. sugar	**1** recipe Trailblazer Biscuit mix (see
1/2 t. mace	Index)

Dehydrate blueberries and bag. Mix sugar and mace. Store separately from cornstarch. Bag Trailblazer Biscuit mix separately.

In-the-field preparation

Rehydrate meat and vegetables. Make hot drinks. Bring sausage, vegetables, stuffing seasoning, 1/3 c. margarine, and 1 1/2 c. water to a boil in the large pot. Cover and boil 5 minutes. Add stuffing bread. Remove from heat. Let it sit, covered, a few minutes, then serve. Reconstitute blueberries on the lid of the eggplant. Prepare biscuit mix according to the recipe, but instead of forming biscuits, spread in skillet and bake with a lid fire for 40–45 minutes. After the biscuit dough is cooked and blueberries are completely rehydrated, bring blueberries and sugar mixture to boil in 1 c. water. Mix cornstarch with 1 T. water in small bowl. When blueberries are boiling, add cornstarch mixture and boil 1 minute, stirring constantly. Remove from heat. Scoop out the center of the biscuit, reserving bread. Be sure to leave at least a 1/2 inch of bread in the bottom of the skillet. Pour blueberries into the center. Crumble bread on top. Serve.

    AS AN OPTION *car camping or on float trips, take frozen sausage and fresh vegetables and fresh, canned, or frozen blueberries in an ice chest. For backpacking and horse packing trips, no adaptation is needed, unless you want to substitute canned blueberry pie filling for fruit, sugar, and cornstarch.*

    SPECIAL: Goat Camp Cheese (start tonight for tomorrow, see in day four's menu).

DAY FOUR MENU

Breakfast

Buttermilk Oatmeal Biscuits
Goat Camp Cheese
Dried Fruit
Coffee

Trail Lunch

Refried Beans (Canned) Spread on Tortillas
Fresh Fruit
Molasses Cookies

Dinner

Goat Flats Grub
Glacier Ice Cream (or Iceless Cream)
Tea

DAY FOUR

Cheese has been around for four thousand years, the result of a happy accident of a long-ago desert traveler. An Arab merchant stored a supply of milk in a bag made out of a sheep's stomach. Rennet, a natural part of the animal's stomach lining, caused curds to form in a watery substance called whey. At the end of the day, when he sat down to drink his milk, he found cheese. It satisfied his hunger, and the whey eased his thirst. Pioneer cooks made rennet by cleaning out a calf's stomach, being sure to leave any pieces of curd (the last milk eaten by the calf) inside. They next soaked the stomach in a quart of water and hung it to dry. The liquid was bottled and used a spoonful or two at a time to make cheese.

Day Four Breakfast recipe

Buttermilk Oatmeal Biscuits

3/4 c. oats
1 c. flour
2 T. powdered buttermilk
3 T. sugar
1/2 t. nutmeg

1 t. baking powder
1/2 t. baking soda
1 t. salt
2 T. margarine

Mix and bag all ingredients except margarine.

Goat Camp Cheese

4 c. goat milk
1/2 tablet rennet

1 t. salt

Pack rennet tablet and a shaker of salt. If no producing doe will accompany you on the journey, take along an extra 1/2 lb. of cheddar cheese. NOTE: powdered or canned milk will not react to rennet and let curds form.

In-the-field preparation

Dissolve rennet in 1/4 c. cold water. Set aside. Heat milk in the smaller pot over a low fire until just barely warm to the touch. No steam should be rising from milk. If it gets too warm (lukewarm is too warm), remove from heat and cool. When the temperature of the milk is correct, remove from the stove and add rennet solution, stirring well. Cover with a wool shirt or sweater. Leave undisturbed overnight.

In the morning after fixing coffee, put cold water in the large pot. Nest the pot containing the cheese on top of the larger pot. Cut curd in large squares (1 inch). Cook curds, uncovered, over lowest possible heat for 30 minutes. Do not stir for the first 15 minutes. Then stir gently (one counterclockwise circle with the spoon) once every five minutes for the last 15 minutes. Remove from stove. Cover and set aside while preparing biscuit dough. Melt margarine in the skillet. Pour it and enough cold water into dry ingredients to make sticky dough. Form biscuits, patting to about 1/2 inch thick. Bake in the skillet over low heat and a lid fire about 10–12 minutes. Makes 17–18. Drain whey from the cheese, reserving it for a unique drink. Add salt, stir gently, and set aside. Serve cheese over biscuits or, as an option, with honey and dried fruit.

THIS MEAL requires no adaptation (other than substituting cheddar for camp cheese) for any of the other kinds of trips.

On the trail, John points to an established pronghorn path that leads to a spring. Hoof prints left by the herd match those of the goats. These two species share common ancestors. From the goat-antelope genes come a greater tolerance to heat, smoother running and walking gate, and better awareness. French Alpines such as Alpie and the Oberhasli like Bob tolerate heat better than other breeds. Saanens like Julio and Sweet Pea, as well as Saanen-Toggenburg crossbreeds like Newlio and Bonita, have endurance, calm dispositions, and tend to grow larger than other breeds. Then La Manchas such as Menu are the most docile breed. Crossbreeding to obtain these desirable traits, John produces pack goats adapted to cold or warm weather conditions as well as high altitudes. Another advantage of these breeds is their agility when it comes to traveling in high mountain terrain. Goats have a better instinct for traversing snowfields than other pack animals. They test the snow first, and if it sounds hollow, they won't proceed. And unlike us humans, they can walk in as much as three feet of snow without getting bogged down.

Of course, the real reward for snow travel with pack goats comes in the form of ice cream. Lucky travelers on the *Oregon Trail* discovered the ice slough, a natural phenomenon on the route where ice could always be found, even in the height of summer. Therefore many pioneers celebrated the Fourth of July with fresh ice cream. Charles Parke, one emigrant to the Far West, wrote down his recipe for ice cream at the South Pass of the Rockies. He put two quarts of milk in a tin bucket and sweetened it with sugar and peppermint. This bucket went into a wooden bucket, and he packed alternate layers of snow and salt around the tin container. With the aid of a clean stick, he stirred the mixture until it transformed into ice cream so delicious that the whole company decided to fire a salute outside his tent in appreciation, "bursting one gun but injuring no one."

Day Four Dinner Recipes

Goat Flats Grub

1 lb. ground beef

2 yellow squash, sliced thin

1 onion, chopped

1 t. pepper

1 t. garlic powder

3 c. spinach noodles

1/4 c. Parmesan cheese

> *Brown ground beef. Dehydrate meat, squash, and onion. Bag with pepper and garlic powder. Store noodles and cheese in two separate bags.*

Glacier Ice Cream

1 large pot snow

goat milk

1/4 c. sugar

2 T. cocoa

> *Bag sugar and cocoa together. If you won't have a producing doe along, substitute canned or powdered milk.*

In-the-field preparation

Reconstitute meat mixture while heating water for hot drinks. In a covered, large pot, bring meat mixture and 2 c. cold water to a boil. Reduce heat to medium. Cook until food is tender. Add enough water to bring level back up to 2 c, and when mixture is boiling, toss in noodles. Cook until noodles are done and most of the liquid is absorbed. Divide into large bowls. Sprinkle with cheese. Serve. For dessert, fill a large pot with fresh snow. Sprinkle sugar mixture on it. Stir in enough fresh goat milk to create the consistency of ice cream. Serve.

AS AN OPTION on float trips or car camping, freeze meat and take fresh vegetables. Substitute iceless cream (see below). Otherwise, this meal can be carried as is on horse packing and backpacking trips.

Since we aren't anywhere near snow or the ice slough tonight, I make iceless cream instead.

Iceless Cream

1 10 oz. pkg. regular marshmallows

3 c. crispy rice cereal

1/4 c. cocoa

2 T. margarine

goat milk

> *Bag everything separately. If not taking a producing doe, substitute either canned or powdered milk.*

In-the-field preparation

Melt margarine in smaller pot over low heat. Add marshmallows, stirring constantly until melted. Add cocoa, stirring until well blended. Blend in cereal then enough milk to make mixture slushy. Serve.

121

DAY FIVE MENU

Breakfast

Julio Potato Ham Melt

Coffee

Trail Lunch

Tuna (Canned) with Catsup on English Muffins

Assorted Fresh Fruit

Molasses Cookies

Dinner

Sweet Pea's Peachy Favorite

Menu's Treat Teacake

Tea

DAY FIVE

Into the nineteenth century, people persisted in viewing both potatoes and tomatoes as poisonous. Cookbooks warned that each should only be eaten if well cooked. Potatoes were boiled to get rid of the "toxins." People threw out the cooking water, which absorbed the poison they thought caused leprosy. Likewise, the only safe way to eat tomatoes involved cooking them at least three hours to remove the "raw taste." Many settlers believed raw tomatoes caused cancer.

Day Five Breakfast Recipe

Julio Potato Ham Melt

4 slices ham, ground
3 tomatoes, chopped
2 1/4 c. instant mashed potatoes
1 t. salt
1 t. pepper

1 T. parsley flakes
1/4 lb. cheese, chopped
3 T. margarine
goat milk

Dehydrate ham and tomatoes. Bag together. Bag instant potatoes separately from remaining ingredients. As always, keep margarine separate. Substitute 1/4 c. powdered milk if not taking a producing doe.

In-the-field preparation

Rehydrate ham and tomatoes while boiling water for coffee. Bring a large pot containing ham mixture and an additional 3 1/4 c. water to a boil. Simmer until ham mixture is tender. Add milk, seasonings, and instant potatoes. Remove from heat. Stir in cheese. Serve.

AS AN OPTION on float trips or car camping, take frozen ham and fresh tomatoes. Otherwise, this meal needs no adaptation for the other trips.

Early in 1972, the U.S. Forest Service hired John to study a herd of bighorn sheep. He needed a way to transport gear and sensitive scientific equipment into the high country. He'd packed with horses for many years and had a couple of goats trained to pull a cart. Horses, however, couldn't cross boulder fields or climb glaciers to keep up with the bighorns. Goats could. Sure-footed relatives of the sheep family, goats feel as much at home on the mountain peaks of the bighorns' habitat as goats do in the barnyard. Furthermore, they made it possible for John to keep a close eye on his subjects as a goat's eyesight is seven times greater than a human's. When one of his goats stopped and stared at something in the distance, John would put a pair of binoculars between the goat's horns and get a fix on sheep he would have otherwise missed.

Goats also pick their path rather than barging through underbrush or low tree limbs. Handy when carrying things such as microscopes or wine goblets (depending on the occasion) in the panniers. On this trip, we didn't bring fancy crystal or equipment. Instead I pull canned peaches out of the panniers, something more rare than crystal until late in the 1800s. Women literally canned peaches by filling tin cans with peeled, sliced fruit. They poured a syrup made from boiling a pint of sugar in a quart of water for five minutes over the peaches then soldered the covers on the cans. Using a nail, the cooks pierced a small hole in the top to let steam escape and put the cans in a washtub filled with water to just below the tops of the cans. This boiled for five minutes over an open fire, then the cans were removed and sealed with more solder.

Day Five Dinner Recipes

Sweet Pea's Peachy Favorite

1 lb. ground sausage

2 onions, chopped

1 10 oz. pkg. frozen green beans (or 1 lb. fresh), cut

1 t. coriander

1 t. cumin

2 t. cinnamon

1 t. ginger

1 16 oz. can sliced peaches in juice

1/3 c. almond slivers

Brown sausage. Dehydrate meat, onion, and beans. Bag dry foods with spices. Store almonds separately. Pack the canned peaches.

Menu's Treat Teacake

1 2/3 c. flour

1 c. brown sugar, firmly packed

1 t. caraway seeds

1 t cinnamon

1/2 c. candied fruits

1/2 c. margarine

goat milk

Bag first flour ingredients together. Store fruit and margarine separately. If there will be no producing doe on the trip, substitute 1/3 c. powdered milk.

In-the-field preparation

Rehydrate meat mixture. Cover. Bring to a boil in the large pot. Open peaches. Add them to meat, juice and all. Simmer until tender, adding more water as needed to maintain about 2 inches of water in the bottom of the pot. Stir frequently. Add almonds and serve. White eating dinner, melt margarine in the skillet. In a pot, blend flour mixture with candied fruits. Add margarine and enough water to make a stiff dough. Spread in skillet. Cover and bake with a lid fire for 40–50 minutes. Serve with milk or hot tea.

AS AN OPTION *on float trips or car camping, substitute frozen sausage, frozen, fresh, or canned beans, and fresh onion. This meal is suitable for backpacking by dehydrating the peaches and for horse packing as is. Canned beans and peaches can be taken if you don't mind the extra weight.*

CHAPTER FOUR

A WEEK-LONG CAR-CAMPING-TIME TRAVEL EXPERIENCE

Car camping provides a unique backcountry experience. It gives campers the essence of the "great outdoors" without the packs. Car camping also allows food choices not feasible on other types of backcountry trips. I prefer to cook with butter rather than margarine. Car camping with ice chests and a steady supply of ice lets me indulge, as well as allowing me to become a bit more creative with meals. Of course, it depends on where you travel on your car camping expedition. On this particular trip we travel through time rather than through terrain. I knew there were going to be well-stocked grocery stores all along the route, and planned the menu in accord with not only the food preferences of my fellow campers but with loads of fresh seasonal picks available from local markets. I replenished fresh meats, vegetables, fruits, milk, cheeses, etc, throughout the trip instead of beginning with the entire amount of food needed for the trip.

Nonetheless, I still purchase all the potatoes and onions (excluding green onions) before heading on the journey and bag them together in a brown paper bag. Right on the outside of the bag, I note the items and the amounts to be used by day and meal. The same goes for the first couple of days of apples, oranges, lemons, and melons with which I start the trip. I buy all the canned goods, too. Using a permanent marker, I label the tops of the cans with the day and meal they are to be used. The meats I begin the trip with I freeze ahead of time, marking the day and meal on the freezer bags. Also, I wash and dry all the fresh vegetables (except mushrooms) and fruits such as grapes and berries with which I begin the trip and bag them in plastic bags especially designed to keep vegetables fresh. These bags get marked same as the potato/onion bag. (A special note, I prefer to purchase lettuce by the bunch however, you may find it more convenient to buy prepared salad or lettuce in bags. If so, transfer them to vegetable storage bags. They'll keep better.) As with other trips, the recipes feed three to four people. Also, if you campers want two sandwiches instead of one, double the recipe. If they only want one egg for breakfast instead of two, cut the recipe by the appropriate amount. If your group drinks milk with every meal, buy accordingly.

If our destination had been as far into the backcountry as our vehicle is allowed to travel, then preparations would call for ice chests stocked for the first couple of days and a combination of canned and dehydrated ingredients grouped by day and meal for the remainder of the trip. As with all the other types of trips, I bring extra meals and cooking fuel as well as plenty of water just in case.

Of course, car camping means I also get to bring a few luxuries from my home kitchen. A cutting board and one of my favorite all-purpose kitchen knives are the first items to get packed in my kitchen box. A basket steamer for vegetables also goes with me, as does a real rolling pin, biscuit cutters, and an old-fashioned camp coffeepot. I toss in a couple of thermoses as well. When I make coffee and tea in the morning, I fill the thermoses for hot drinks along the way if traveling in high altitude where it can snow every month of the year, or cold drinks if I'm journeying through a hot climate. I like to cook with wine (and serve it with meals when appropriate to the adults; the kids get juice, milk, or tea), so a good corkscrew goes in the box as well. I do, however, compromise and pack plastic wineglasses. There's a reason why women traveling the *Oregon Trail* carefully packed their good china and crystal deep in the wagon and served meals on tin plates, and they drank out of tin cups during the journey. But even more important, I get to take a small folding table. It makes a great cooking prep work space at camp and provides a stable spot for another indulgence, my tailgate oven and propane fuel canisters. Each canister gives me six hours of baking time, and I don't have to worry about camping in areas that allow fires in order to bake. To me, this is the epitome of luxury in the backcountry! Well, part of it. It's hard to beat sitting in a comfy camp chair, your feet propped up on the ice chest, and a glass of Merlot in hand while you listen to the elk bugle.

FOOD FOR THE TRAIL

When you are car camping, think snacks. While driving, I ensure everybody has ready access to water, juice, and ice tea (or thermoses of hot drinks). Snacks usually take the form of mixed nuts, sunflower seeds, pine nuts, cheese chunks, sliced pepperoni or summer sausage, and carrot and celery sticks. Poll your fellow campers on their snack preferences and plan accordingly.

SUPPLY LIST (7 DAYS)

Baking Staples

1 5 lb. sack flour
1 5 lb. sack sugar
1 2 lb. sack cornmeal
1 1b. dark brown sugar
1 qt. bottle vegetable oil
1 small bottle olive oil
1 container baking powder

1 container baking soda
1 container sea salt
1 box cornstarch
1 bag semisweet chocolate chips
1 container Italian bread crumbs
1 bottle almond extract

Crackers/Cereals/Chips

1 pkg. croutons
1 bag corn chips
1 bag potato chips
1 box graham crackers
1 box rye crackers

1 box buttery crackers
1 box whole wheat crackers
1 box shredded wheat
1 box cornflakes

Dried Fruit/Vegetables/Nuts (in addition to trail foods)

1 2 oz. pkg. pecans
2 2 oz. pkg. almond slivers

1 bag hazelnuts
1 box chopped dates

Fresh Fruit

3 lemon
1 orange
3 melons (I usually take 2 cantaloupe, 1 honeydew)
4 kiwis
8 nectarines
12 plums
12 apricots

9 peaches
1 green apple
2 bunches seedless grapes
1 pt. blackberries
1 pt. container raspberries
1 pt. fresh blueberries
1 qt. dark red or black cherries
2 qt. fresh strawberries

Fresh Vegetables

6 onions
3 Bermuda onions
4 medium yellow potatoes
4 cloves fresh garlic
2 bunches green onions
2 tomatoes
1 16 oz. pkg. cherry or grape tomatoes
12 radishes
1 2 lb. bag carrots
2 bunches celery
3 cucumber
1 2 oz. piece of ginger root
1 3 oz. pkg. bean sprouts
1 4 oz. container alfalfa sprouts

10 ears corn
1 bunch spinach
2 bunch leaf lettuce
1 bunch buttercrunch lettuce
1 yellow summer squash
2 zucchini
1 eggplant
1/2 lb. green beans
1 yellow sweet pepper
5 red bell pepper
3 green bell pepper
1 bunch fresh broccoli
1 8 oz. box mushrooms

Canned Goods

1 10.75 oz. can tomato soup
1 15 oz. can sweet peas
1 18.5 oz. can split pea soup
1 29 oz. can chopped tomatoes

2 29 oz. can whole pealed tomatoes
1 6 oz. (dry weight) can black olives
1 2.25 oz. can of sliced or minced black
   olive

Breads/Baked Goods

1 pkg. breadsticks
kaiser rolls
1 loaf rye bread
1 loaf sour dough bread
1 loaf white bread

1 loaf whole wheat bread
2 baguette of French or Italian bread
4 sponge shortcakes
1 pound cake
1 loaf-shaped angel food cake

Meat/Milk/Butter/Cheese/Yogurt/Eggs

1 lb. deli sliced ham
1 lb. ham
1 lb. sliced pimiento loaf
4 slices roast beef (thin deli cut)
4 slices roast beef, 1/4 inch thick
4 thin slices of veal
1 lb. thick sliced bacon

2 links andouille or hot sausage
2 5 oz. cans white albacore tuna
1 5 oz. can chicken breast
2 12 oz. can chicken
1 3.75 oz. can oysters
1 5 oz. can shrimp
3 lb. butter

1 small container cream cheese
1 small container sour cream
1 4 oz. container light cream
1 small container cottage cheese
1 gal. milk (for cooking and putting on cereal only, add more for drinking with meals)
8 8 oz. assorted yogurts with fruit
2 8 oz. plain yogurt

1/2 lb. slices of cheddar cheese
2 lb. sharp cheddar cheese
1/2 lb. sliced swiss cheese
1 bag shredded cheese
1 8 oz. container Parmesan cheese
3 dozen egg
1 qt. vanilla ice cream (purchase on the trip)

Rice/Noodles

1 12 oz. pkg. veggie spirals pasta

2 lb. rice

Sauces and Other Mixes/Drinks/Specialty Items

1 liter bottle root beer
1 can club soda
1 lb. coffee
50 assorted tea bags
3 bottles assorted juices (I usually take 1 orange, 1 grapefruit, 1 cranberry)
8 assorted juice boxes
1 qt. bottle apple cranberry juice
1 qt. bottle Limeade
1 1.2 oz. pkg. Béarnaise Sauce
1 1.2 oz. pkg. Hollandaise Sauce
1 jar Dijon mustard
1 8 oz. container cocoa
1 jar raspberry preserves
1 pt. brandy
1 12 oz. bottle of good Ale

1 small bottle sherry
1 bottle claret
3 bottles Merlot (or favorite)
1 small jar green olives stuffed with pimentos
1 small jar sweet pickle relish
1 jar capers
1 bottle reconstituted lemon juice
1 bottle balsamic vinegar
1 bottle wine vinegar
1 bottle Italian dressing
1 bottle ranch dressing
2 squeeze bottles of mayonnaise
1 roll tin foil
1 box toothpicks
2 rolls paper towels

Spices

1 container sweet basil
1 container black pepper
1 container dried parsley
1 container dry mustard
1 container garlic powder
1 container ground cinnamon

1 container stick cinnamon
1 container mace
1 container nutmeg
1 container paprika
1 container rosemary

DAY ONE MENU

Breakfast

Gold Strike Morning Cereal
Yogurt with Fresh Nectarines
Car Camp Coffee
Juice

Lunch

Tea Triangles
Cheese Ballot
Morris Morsels
Tea

Dinner

Miner's Delight Salmon
Gold Dust Salad
Boom Bust Biscuits
Peaches and Plums
Wine, Tea and/or Milk

DAY ONE

The calendar says June, but the cool breeze that accompanies sunrise feels more like early spring. As the orange glow turns into golden sunshine, however, the morning chill quickly passes. Eager to begin our adventure, Mandy and her two teenagers, Linda and Connor, lobby for driving straight from the Riverton, Wyoming, airport to the campground near South Pass City where our seven-day car camping trek launches. We've been planning this journey since last year and had reserved campground spots to suit our itinerary. An ER nurse, Mandy anticipates enjoying a relaxing time with her kids and her old friend, being outdoors as much as possible, and not having to deal with cooking. She's doing the dishes, and the kids will be setting up and breaking down camp while I cook and drive. Linda, who wants to become a social studies teacher, can't wait to see tangible history. Rock hound Connor longs to get the lay of the land, literally. He knows geologists consider the state a geological paradise, and one rock in particular drew thousands to the encampment that would become South Pass City—gold.

South Pass City, now a state historic site, sits on a plateau at the southern end of the Wind River Range, near the Rocky Mountain pass from which the town took its name. Granites and schists of the pre-Cambrian age form the backbone of what the locals simply call the Winds, while, as noted in 1911 by state geologist Claude E. Jamison, "Lying uncomfortably [*sic*] upon these are Cambrian sandstones and conglomerates." Regardless, words fail in attempting to describe the awe-inspiring beauty of this mountain range.

Prospectors discovered gold in the South Pass area in 1842. Although the streams in the region saw quite a bit of panning, it wasn't until 1867 when disheartened miners who went bust in California tried their hand along the South Pass on their way back to the States that the rich veins revealed themselves. Henry Reedal made the first mining claim on what became known as the Carissa Lode. A hard-rock operation, the Carissa Mine produced over six million dollars' worth of the coveted ore in just a four hundred-foot shaft and set off a boom. In March 1868, *Scientific American* stated that South Pass City sported eighty houses, eight businesses, and seven hundred residents. The State of Wyoming purchased the mine site and nine historic structures located on 201 acres in 2003 and raced time in restoration and renovation designed to protect the structures.

We eat our simple breakfast of cereal, yogurt, and fruit in the shadow of the Carissa Mine. (Since our trip, the main building has opened to the public for touring and a museum.) Linda and Connor have cranberry juice. Mandy and I indulge in a rich cup of java. An article run in *The Cultivator* in 1840 suggested that the best coffee required roasting the beans, grinding them, and immediately pouring boiling water over the grounds. It should be boiled for twenty-five minutes as "longer than this is prejudicial" then cleared or clarified (settling the grounds). This article suggested using a fish skin the size of a shilling or brewing the grounds in a filter made from clean flannel cloth. The grounds were tied in the flannel and dropped in the boiling water like a modern-day tea bag. A much better option than a fish skin! Either way, once "tolerably clear," the "goodness of coffee" then depended "on the quality of cream and sugar used with it. *Skimmed milk* and rich coffee are incompatible." Mandy agrees and adds a splash of cream and a spoon of raw sugar to her coffee. I drizzle in some cream, but the sugar is all for Mandy.

Day One Breakfast Recipe

Gold Strike Morning Cereal

4 c. corn flakes   **1** c. hazelnuts, chopped
4 c. shredded wheat   **1/2** gal. milk
   Mix all ingredients except milk together in a large bowl and bag. Pack the milk in the ice chest.

Yogurt with Fresh Nectarines

2 8 oz. plain yogurt   **4** fresh nectarines
   Pack container of yogurt in the ice chest. Bag nectarines.

Car Camp Coffee

1 T. ground coffee per person (for   **1/4** t. ground cinnamon
   two cups of coffee)   (not per person)
   Bag together.

In-the-field preparation

Add 2 c. water for every coffee drinker. Place paper filter in the basket. Add coffee cinnamon mix. Bring to a boil on high heat. Reduce to low (but still perking) and simmer for 5 minutes. Meanwhile, divide the cereal mixture between everybody's bowls. Add desired amount of milk. Quarter and pit the nectarines, dividing them equally into another bowl or plate for each person. Add a scoop of yogurt. Serve.

   THIS MEAL *needs no adaptation for a first morning goat, horse, or float trip. Pre-mix yogurt and pitted fruit and bag for each individual. When backpacking, use powdered milk for the cereal and the coffee sock coffee recipe.*

Within two years of the discovery of the Carissa Lode, over three thousand people flocked to the area. By 1872, however, the boom went bust, and South Pass City resembled a ghost town. Linda thinks the historic site is all about the gold; however, in between the boom and the bust, the city saw some rich political history.

Our first stop once entering the historic town site is the Esther Morris Museum, a reconstructed building replacing the one that burned down in 1871. It was originally the newspaper office that belonged to Edward A. Slack, Morris's son from her first marriage. Linda knows about Susan B. Anthony, Matilda Joslyn Gage, Elizabeth Cady Stanton, and Seneca Falls Convention, but she's never heard of Morris or the role South Pass City played in women's suffrage.

In 1870, Morris made national history by becoming the first woman to hold office as a justice of the peace, serving up justice in her bailiwick of 460 people for eight and a half months. Historians disagree about the number of cases she tried, but none argue over her record as justice of the peace. No higher court ever overturned any of her twenty-six to fifty case decisions. Unfortunately, regardless of her exemplary record, Morris received no reappointment and subsequently retired, but her role in women's suffrage would change and grow with the passage of years.

After his newspaper office burned down, Slack left South Pass City and worked as an editor of the *Cheyenne Sun*. In an 1890 issue, he began referring to Morris as the Mother of Woman Suffrage. Then a historian named Grace Raymond Hebard, who would later proclaim the "honor of being a personal friend of Mrs. Esther Morris," seized upon this slogan, writing in the 1913 *Laramie Republican* that women enfranchisement "owed its existence to Colonel William H. Bright and Mrs. Esther Morris, who thus became respectively the father and mother of equal suffrage . . . . These two minds acting upon each other were the flint and the steel which produced the spark that lighted the torch of real democracy." Bright, a mine owner and saloon keeper in South Pass City, was elected to Wyoming's First Territorial Legislature. Also in 1913, Hebard wrote about Bright's role in suffrage in the *Journal of American History*, crediting him as saying that although women like his mother and his wife should be allowed the vote, "he was helped in his convictions and fortified for the battle he expected to fight by the opinions of his wife and the acquaintance of one of his townspeople, Mrs. Esther Morris, who has since earned the unchallenged right to the title of 'The Mother of Woman Suffrage.'"

Forty-three years after the Wyoming Territorial Legislature voted women's suffrage into law, H. G. Nickerson, the candidate who lost to Bright in that first election, published a letter in the February 14, 1919, *Wyoming State Journal*. In it he claimed both he and Bright were among approximately forty guests at a tea party hosted by Mrs. Esther Morris at her home in South Pass City a few days prior to the 1869 election. Nickerson wrote, "While sitting at the table Mrs. Morris arose and stated the object of the meeting. She said: 'There are present two opposing candidates for the first legislature of our new territory, one of which is sure to be elected, and we desire here and now to receive from them a public pledge that whichever one is elected will introduce and work for the passage of an act conferring upon the women of our new Territory the right of suffrage.'" Nickerson went on to state, "Of course, we both pledge ourselves as requested, and received the applause of all present . . . Bright, true to his promise, introduced the bill and it became a law."

Many feel Morris was also crucial in setting the stage for women being granted voting privileges in Wyoming in 1869. Wyoming became the first state or territory to grant women's suffrage in the United States. Hence Wyoming's motto is "the Equality State."

By general consensus, we vote its lunch time. Therefore, we meander past the Blacksmith Shop and the Sherlock Garage to a picnic area. Both of these buildings are examples of recycling. Logs for construction were not easily available, so abandoned structures were fair game. The Blacksmith Shop contains logs from Ticknor Store, originally built in 1868. The Sherlock Garage was erected using logs salvaged from town constable Jim Smith's 1868 cabin and the abandoned home belonging to William Carr, the town's butcher during the early 1900s.

In honor of Morris and the infamous tea party she held here, we have our own tea-style lunch with tea, of course! In 1802, a traveler to America complained that "tea-parties were invented by avarice, in order to see company cheap. They give on the other hand occasion for the display of some silver furniture, which flatters the owner's vanity." As for what was served, "They drink warm water; they eat, for the most part, bread smeared with butter. The rule is to drink only two cups. After tea they drink a glass of Madeira-wine." "At a sociable tea-party you sit round a table, and have various articles handed you, to eat, such as cold meat, fish, etc. If these tea-parties were not so stiff, they would be a very good invention to see company at home without much expense." Ironically, the traveler also complained that there were "not many clubs extant, and none at all for political purposes." Such was not the case with Morris's tea party.

Day One Lunch Recipe

Tea Triangles

1 12 oz. can chicken	**1/4** t. ground black pepper
1 T. sweet pickle relish	**2** T. ranch dressing
1/2 small onion, chopped fine	rye bread

Chop onion and bag by itself. Add pepper to pickle relish and bag. Bag rye bread separately. Pack bottle of ranch dressing and can of chicken.

Cheese Ballot

1 c. cream cheese, softened
1 T. dried parsley
1/4 c. pecans, chopped fine

2 T. red wine
1/2 c. buttery crackers, pulverized

Blend cream cheese, parsley, pecans, and wine in a food processor. Add a splash more wine if needed to get the mixture started blending. Pulverize crackers in a blender. Form cheese mixture into small balls and roll in cracker crumbs, coating the ball completely so they aren't sticky. Bag. Pack in the ice chest.

Morris Morsels

1 loaf-shaped angel food cake, cut into squares

4 T. raspberry preserves
4 T. semisweet chocolate chips

Cut the cake into square pieces and bag. Bag the chocolate chips. Pack the jar of preserves.

In-the-field preparation

Open the can of chicken and drain. Mix it into the bag containing the relish mixture. Add enough ranch dressing to make it a spreadable consistency. Cut bread into triangles and spread with chicken mixture. Serve with cheese ballots on the side. For dessert, top cake squares with a spoonful of preserves and some chocolate chips. Serve. If a cool day, boil water and add tea bags. Otherwise, serve ice tea.

NOTE: There should be Tea Triangles sandwich filling leftover. Store it in a plastic bag in the ice chest to be included in the Bedroll Burgers recipe for part of tomorrow's lunch. For goat and horse trips, use a smaller can of chicken and don't have any leftovers.

THIS MEAL needs no adaptation for a first day lunch on a float trip. For horse or goat trips, make the sandwiches ahead of time and bag individually. Cheese Ballots work better as a spread on crackers for these trips. Choose another lunch option for backpacking.

After lunch, we cross the "avenue" to the Gold Mining Interpretive Center. Originally the building housed Jim Smith's mercantile business. The exhibits put the gold mining process in perspective. Connor would have gladly spent the rest of the day pouring over the displays.

The afternoon winds down with us wandering through the rest of the thirty-nine-acre, open-air museum, the scent of nineteenth-century gold dust still lingering on the breeze. Connor finds it ironic that the Exchange Bank, opened in 1868 to assess and purchase prospectors' raw gold, should become the Exchange Saloon and Card Room said to be frequented by none other than legendary bank robber Butch Cassidy. The paradox of the Sweatwater County Jail from the 1870s receiving a face-lift in the 1880s to become a schoolroom complete with pink painted walls and the alphabet still visible over the door amuses Mandy, while Linda and Connor consider it no contradiction at all.

The city saw many restaurants over the years, including the one added onto the very prestigious South Pass Hotel that sported front-door stagecoach service and for a while a post office in the hotel. Seeing the dining room reminds me of a story about Mrs. Baker. When the claim four fellows named Miner's Delight "panned out" and they could afford it, they hired Mrs. Baker away from the "Salmon River dining tables" to cook exclusively for them, paying her $75 a month. But come spring 1868, Dagmar Mariager recalled that Mrs. Baker started an eatery in a tent that "did a thriving business at one dollar per meal—and the bill of fare was neither very varied nor sumptuous, but the cooking was good and carefully seen to, and the result was good and wholesome food." Strapped miners could get a cold lunch "in their pockets" by presenting themselves at the entrance and purchasing crackers, cheese, various kinds of canned fruits, sardines, canned oysters, dried salmon, "sugar of lemon," and "red-jacket bitters," as well as buckskin gloves, cartridges, plug tobacco, cigars, and colored socks "all for a good, round price, and be glad of the chance to get them." We, however, dine on Miner's Delight Salmon that isn't dried. My folding table makes a great work space for chopping vegetables for the salad and rolling out the biscuits.

Day One Dinner Recipes

Miner's Delight Salmon

4 fresh salmon fillets

1 fresh lemon

1/2 t. course ground black pepper

1/4 c. water

If using frozen fillets, bag them together and place in the top of the ice chest so that they will thaw by dinnertime the first night. If using fresh fillets, purchase them no sooner than the day prior to the trip and pack them in the ice the morning of your trip. Bag the lemon and pepper separately.

Gold Dust Salad

1/2 head of lettuce

1/2 of a small Bermuda onion, chopped

2 radishes, sliced thin

1 carrot, sliced thin

1/2 yellow sweet pepper, cut in strips

2 stalks celery, chopped

1 c. croutons

1/2 c. cheddar cheese, shredded

ranch dressing (or choice of salad dressings)

Wash and dry lettuce. Shred it and bag. Prepare radishes, carrot, sweet pepper, and celery and bag together. Bag onion separately. Also bag croutons and cheese individually. Pack dressing(s).

Boom Bust Biscuits

2 2/3 c. flour

1 t. salt

1 t. baking powder

1 t. baking soda

3/4 c. cottage cheese

4 T. butter

Bag together all ingredients except 1/3 c. of flour, cottage cheese, and butter. Reserve the 1/3 c. flour for rolling out biscuits.

In-the-field preparation

In a large bowl, cut 4 T. butter into biscuit mix. Add 3/4 c. cottage cheese. Mix just enough to form the dough. If dough is too thick, add a bit of water. It too thin, add some of the reserve flour. Flour the cutting board and rolling pin. Roll out dough to 1/2 inch thickness. Cut out biscuits with the biscuit cutter and put in a greased pan. Bake at 350°F for 10–15 minutes.

Meanwhile, cut the lemon in half and squeeze juice into a skillet. Add the 1/4 c. water. Arrange fillets in the pan, sprinkle the pepper on top. Cover. Cook over medium heat for 10–15 minutes, turning once. Mix salad ingredients in a large bowl. Once biscuits are golden brown, serve with butter. Pour wine and tea or milk accordingly. For dessert, pit and quarter 3 peaches and 4 plums.

THIS MEAL needs no adaptation for a first night dinner on float trips. Use canned salmon and canned fruit in place of fresh on horse and goat trips. Replace salad with carrot and celery sticks. Substitute 3/4 c. shredded Cheddar cheese, 1/4 c. powdered milk, and enough water to make a stiff dough for the cottage cheese. Choose another dinner option for backpacking.

DAY TWO MENU

Breakfast

Ghost Town Ham Hash

Yogurt

Pacific City Cocoa

Coffee

Lunch

Bedroll Burgers

Plums

Juice boxes

Dinner

Sinks Canyon Supper

Rise Bread

Climber Cake

Wine, Tea, and/or Milk

DAY TWO

Connor rises early and meanders through the sagebrush looking for rocks. Linda pauses from stuffing her sleeping bag in its travel sack to watch a couple on horseback trot down the dirt road that leads toward Atlantic City, South Pass's sister city. Unlike South Pass City, Atlantic City isn't a ghost town. The town's inhabitants, however, have managed to retain much of the gold fever charm in the homes and businesses. I hand Mandy a cup of coffee and wave her away from helping as I get breakfast started. According to a disgruntled husband, using the pseudonym of "Q. in the corner," complained that "this dogged obstinacy of the cook" for "not putting on her pot, at least one hour sooner than she does, as one of the 'greatest ills that flesh is heir to.'" By not doing so, his "wife dooms him to endure the calamity to come home on Sunday with a bevy of friends, all 'hungry as hawks'" only to find that the "early Yorks—new potatoes," and the "very fine ham *half done*! cabbage *half boiled*!" for not following "old Miss Nelly Blackburn, who knew all things, and whose good sense was derived solely from the '*Book of Nature*'" and boiling dinner for "*two hours and a half*!" All the while he lamented, "Everyone knows that certain things *are ruined by being over-done*." Cookbooks prior to the late 1800s, however, warned, "If the water once relaxes from its heat, the goodness of the potato is sure to be affected" adversely and insisted that "if not eaten the very moment it is boiled, the potato is worth nothing."

Day Two Breakfast Recipe

Ghost Town Ham Hash

1 lb. ham, grated
4 medium whole yellow potatoes
1/2 green bell pepper

1/2 red bell pepper
5 green onions, chopped
1/4 c. vegetable oil

    Grate ham, bag, and freeze until ready to pack in ice chest. Chop green onions (tails too). Bag and store in refrigerator until ready to pack in ice chest. Leave peppers and potatoes whole until ready to use. Unless you plan to peel the potatoes, scrub them and make certain they are completely dry before packing them in a paper bag in the car. Pack the peppers in the ice chest. Remember to pack a plastic container of vegetable oil.

Pacific City Cocoa

4 c. milk
4 T. sugar

4 T. cocoa
2 t. almond extract

    Mix cocoa and sugar together and bag. Remember to pack milk and almond extract.

In-the-field preparation

Brew Car Camp Coffee (see Car Camping Day One recipe). Chop peppers and set aside. Grate potatoes. Heat vegetable oil in a frying pan. Add potatoes, ham, green onions, and peppers. Cover and cook over medium heat until golden brown or desired crispness, flipping once. Serve with yogurt on the side. Heat milk and cocoa mixture in a covered saucepan on low, stirring frequently. Do not let the milk boil. When hot, remove from heat and add almond extract. Pour into mugs and serve.

THIS MEAL needs no adaptation for a second day breakfast on goat, horse, or float trips, however substitute powered milk for fresh in the cocoa. For backpacking, dehydrate ham and vegetables and cook in margarine. Skip the yogurt.

After a leisurely breakfast, we leave the dust of South Pass City behind and head over to what the locals refer to as the Loop Road. It is the scenic summer shortcut that switchbacks over the mountains that stand between South Pass City and the town of Lander. Snow closes the Loop Road by late autumn. It doesn't reopen until late spring. Heading up the switchbacks, we pass stunning mountain vistas and hit a few rough spots on the road.

The trailhead for Silas Lake, our day hike destination, sits by the south edge of the Fiddlers Lake Campground. I pull into the parking area that overlooks the small lake. A breeze whispers through the pine forest on the other side of the lake and ripples the water. While Mandy and the kids fill water bottles from the gallon jug in the trunk, I pack lunch into our day packs.

After we sign in at the trailhead, listing our destination of Lower Silas Lake, we head down the well-defined path that takes off to the right, immediately winding into a forest of limber pines. Square blazes notched into the yellow inner bark mark the route along the way. The pines' pungent scent fills the air. Recognizable by their five-needle clusters, these limber pines produce a nut which squirrels and chipmunks like to collect for winter. Mountain men learned from the Shoshones how to spot and raid such caches for a delicious meal. Of course, these fellows had to keep one eye out for bears doing the same thing! The indigenous peoples also taught explorers how to turn the sticky pine sap into a disinfectant for scratches and other minor wounds and to smear it on their skin as an insect repellent (something I know we'll need at Silas Lake).

Within a short distance along the trail, a small pond appears off to the left, followed by a marshy meadow on the right, both created by Fiddlers Creek. Linda excitedly points out fresh deer tracks in the mud at the pond's edge. Deer graze on the lush grasses early in the morning and around dusk. On the far side a wood duck hugs the rim of water, a white-patched eye forever watching us.

Back on the path, the pines provide a cool canopy from the strengthening sun. A low undergrowth of whortleberry sprouts out of the litter of brown needles, dappling the ground with green. Among a mingling of horseshoe and hiking boot prints a fine dust rises and settles with each of our footfalls. Purple and pink aspen daisies, dots of color beside the trail, shake off the dust in a slight breeze.

Behind them sits a pile of gray granite, looking like it has been stacked there by some long-forgotten giant. Connor announces that granitic bedrock makes up the core of the Wind River, Washakie, Owl Creek, and Teton mountains. This material originated as an accumulation of sediments and lavas on an ancient ocean floor about 3.5 billion years ago. Heat and pressure metamorphosed the muck into the granitic rock that can be seen in the high peaks of the Winds. Glaciers once forced enormous boulders or clusters of rock down from high elevations. Hikers in the Winds can still see glacier scaring on the rocks. As it is characteristic of debris deposited by glacial melting, this surface pile before us reminds us of the power manifested by shifting glacier fields.

Farther on, we hear the sound of a brook gurgles over rocks and roots. It grows louder, its course intersecting with the path. But nature furnishes plenty of stepping stones to make a dry shoe crossing for us. Bluebells wave silent chimes along its banks. Everything from the largest elk to the tiniest pica enjoy this forage, including several salad-starved backpackers I know. Yarrow's small white flowers also bloom near the creek. Their strangely pleasant scent teases our noses.

From the creek, a steady incline leads us up to 9,600 feet elevation. Along the way, the forest opens up onto a view of the Wind River Range sloping down into the actual South Pass. A huge boulder of granite with a flat tablelike top offers a great place to sit and absorb the landscape. While Connor examines the boulder, the rest of us take a break and rehydrate. Mandy knows how important it is to drink lots of water and take it easy in higher elevations, especially for lowlanders.

All remains quiet around us, yet nature speaks loudly. Wind rustles the pines, sounding like the taffeta and satin gowns of Civil War era dancers swirling about a ballroom. Flies and bees *beeuzzzby*. Clouds drift through the brilliant turquoise sky. Red squirrels scold us for this trespass from their lofts of safety high in the trees. The scarlet-accented head of a downy woodpecker bobs as it hammers into the pine bark, sending a faint echo bouncing between the surrounding pines. Mountain chickadees add a chorus of high-pitched *tsick a dee dee dees*.

After chugging down some more water, we move on. Up ahead the trail divides. Silas Lake goes to the right. The fork to the left takes travelers to Gustave Lake or on to Christina Lake. I tell Mandy and the kids about a worn-out hiker who once

scratched "100 more miles" into the wooden sign next to the mileage for Christina Lake. We get a good giggle out of that, but nine miles can seem like one hundred in the high-altitude backcountry, especially for those ill-prepared to deal with thin atmosphere, strong sun rays, and staying hydrated. The Popo Agie Wilderness boundary follows immediately the forks in the trail. Popo Agie, pronounced pō-PŌ-zŭh, means "head water" in the Crow language.

A couple of muddy drainages out of Silas Creek present some rock hopping farther along. We circle to the left at the second one to avoid getting our feet soaked. Lots of downed, decaying trees provide an adequate walkway, however. The trail loops down to the lake along a rock-strewn path. Nearby, Silas Creek roars into the lake.

As with all good fishing spots, the mosquitoes can get bad. As long as insect repellent comes with the menu, Lower Silas Lake makes a nice place to picnic, therefore I came prepared. We spray up before locating a cozy spot near the confluence of the creek and lake to bask in the sunlight and munch on our sandwiches. In the 1840s, obtaining good flour for bread required some work. As smut injured the wheat to be milled into flour, cooks had to wash wheat one bushel at a time by filling a tub with freshwater drawn from a well or creek and quickly scrubbed the wheat grain with her hands or stirred this well with a stick. She repeated this process until the water was no longer dirty, usually two or three times. The reason she had to act quickly was to prevent the grains from soaking up water. Once the wheat was thoroughly washed, the cook spread the grains out on a clean bedsheet covering a board in a sunny location. She turned the grains by hand every couple of hours until the wheat dried. If the weather cooperated, the wheat dried in a day. Cookbooks of this period suggested that as fresh milled flour made the sweetest bread, to not mill more than one or two bushels at a time.

Day Two Lunch Recipe

Bedroll Burgers

4 slices roast beef (thin deli cut)
Tea Triangles filling (leftover from
    yesterday)
1 4 oz. container alfalfa sprouts

lettuce leaves
kaiser rolls
4 T. Dijon mustard

> *Have the deli put paper between the slices of roast beef and repackage four slices separated by the paper in a plastic bag. Freeze until ready to pack in the ice chest. Wash lettuce. Pat dry with paper towels and store in a zippered plastic bag especially designed for vegetables. Pack rolls, sprouts, lettuce, and 8 plums when ready to leave. Unless you're traveling in a hot climate zone, the bread shouldn't need to be packed in the ice chest. Pack mustard.*

In-the-field preparation

> *Slice kaiser rolls in half and spread with mustard. Scoop 2 to 3 spoonfuls of Tea Triangles filling onto each slice of roast beef. Add 1/4 of the sprouts. Top with a leaf of lettuce. Roll up the roast beef and place in the Kiser roll. Serve.*
>
>   **THIS MEAL** *needs no adaptation for a second day lunch on float trips. Choose another option for lunch on all other types of trips.*

We no sooner finish eating, then it starts sprinkling while the sun continues to beam down on us. It rarely amounts to more than having to wipe a few drops off your dark glasses, though. So we just laugh it off and continue eating lunch. Mandy asks if the kids want to extend our day hike by circling around the edge of the lake and picking up the trail to Tomahawk Lake, approximately another mile, or head upstream to Upper Silas Lake, one and a half miles farther. Linda decides she's perfectly happy right where she is, watching the fish surfacing to try to catch the mosquitoes. Mindful that the extended route would almost double our hiking time and the mileage and being anxious to see Sinks Canyon, Connor votes for heading back.

    Geologists state that the upper quarter of the canyon consists of pre-Cambrian granite of the Louis Lake Formation. The lower canyon walls where we will be camping are comprised of Paleozoic limestone, dolomite, and sandstone. Coming into the canyon from the Loop Road, we reach "the Sinks" as its known locally first. The Sinks received its name from the Middle Fork of the Popo Agie River, disappearing (it literally sinks) into a porous limestone cave about halfway through the canyon. A quarter mile farther, it emerges into a large, calm pool called "the Rise," on the opposite side of the canyon. The water takes a little over two hours to travel that quarter mile. Something odd occurs at the Rise, however. More water comes out of it than flowed into the Sinks, plus the water of the Rise is warmer than that of the Sinks. Recently, undergraduates from the University of Missouri that runs summer programs through their geology field camp near Sinks Canyon State Park, conducted a dye-tracing experiment that showed the water flow between the cave and the Rise hadn't changed in the twenty-three years since the similar dye experiment carried out by the U.S. Geological Survey. Connor wants to attend the University of Missouri because of this field camp. He thinks their environmental geology that incorporates hydrogeology and geophysics into the curriculum will be fantastic.

Of course, at the moment, Connor wants to go spelunking in the cave. His plea meets a resounding no from his mother. Besides, the afternoon is disappearing as fast as the river into the Sinks, and the rest of us want to see the Rise before checking into the Sinks Canyon State Park campground that's on a first-come-first-get system. From the overlook deck, we can peer straight down into the Rise. Mammoth trout, the size to start anyone interested in fishing salivating, lazily swim around in the warm water. These are not fish farm trout. They got here all on their own. Since people can and do buy fish food for them, the trout are always hanging around the Rise, ready to put on a great show for visitors.

Elinore Rupert Stewart, a woman who homesteaded in the early 1900s not too far from this area by Wyoming standards, wrote to a friend in Denver, Colorado, "This air is so tonic that one gets delightfully hungry." It is certainly true. As we set up camp, I throw together appetizers of cream cheese on biscuits from last night's dinner topped with nuts from the snack bag. When Stewart worked as the housekeeper for the rancher she would later marry, she considered herself exceptionally fortunate that she had seven cows to milk. The sale of the butter she churned went toward the purchase of flour with which to bake biscuits and breads.

Day Two Dinner Recipes

Sinks Canyon Supper

1 large eggplant, sliced

1 medium onion, chopped

1/2 red bell pepper, chopped

1/2 green bell pepper, chopped

1 29 oz. can whole pealed tomatoes

1/4 c. plus 2 T. vegetable oil

1/2 c. flour

1/4 c. Parmesan cheese (dried that comes in a plastic bottle similar to other spices)

1/4 t. black pepper

1 can club soda

Mix flour, Parmesan cheese, and black pepper together and bag in a gallon-size bag. Leave vegetables whole until ready to prepare dinner. Pack eggplant and bell peppers in the ice chest when ready to leave. Pack onion in a paper bag in the car. Pack canned tomatoes, club soda, and oil.

Rise Bread

1 baguette of French or Italian bread

4 T. butter

1 T. garlic powder

1 T. sweet basil

Mix garlic and basil and bag. Pack butter in the ice chest when ready to leave. Pack bread.

Climber Cake

4 slices of pound cake

4 peaches

Slice pound cake and bag. Wash and dry peaches. Pack them in ice chest when ready to leave.

In-the-field preparation

Slice the eggplant into 1/4 inch thick slices. Pour soda into a large bowl. Add eggplant slices. Meanwhile, slice onion and bell peppers. Sauté onions and bell pepper in 2 T. of oil in a large saucepan. When browned and still firm, add tomatoes. Simmer on low for five minutes to heat thoroughly. Heat the 1/4 c. oil in a large skillet. Toss eggplant one slice at a time in the flour-cheese mixture (don't dry them before shaking in the flour). Cook covered over medium heat until browned. You may need to add more oil if it becomes absorbed in the flour mixture. Flipping once to cook both sides. When done, remove with a slotted spatula and drain on paper towels. Preheat oven to 350°F degrees. Slice bread to desired thickness, spread butter on top, and sprinkle with garlic powder mixture. Wrap pieces in tin foil and place in the oven to heat. Place eggplant on the plate first and ladle tomato mixture on top. Sprinkle with more Parmesan cheese if desired and serve with bread.

Serve wine and/or tea. When ready for dessert, place pound cake slices on individual plates, peal and slice peaches and arrange on top. Serve.

THIS MEAL needs no adaptation for a float trip second night dinner or as a first-night option on goat and horse trips. For backpacking, dehydrate vegetables and soak eggplant in water rather than club soda in the field.

SPECIAL: For tomorrow's breakfast, after dinner, bring 1 c. rice and 1 c. water to a boil in a covered saucepan over high heat. As soon as it begins to boil, add 2 T. cold water and reduce to low heat. Simmer undisturbed for 30 minutes. If camping in a hot climate or bear country, store in a plastic bag in the ice chest when cooled. AS AN OPTION, cook rice at home and freeze in a plastic bag when cool. Toss it frozen into the ice chest before leaving.

SPECIAL: For tomorrow's lunch, prepare Crowheart Butte Cold Fruit Soup after dinner.

Crowheart Butte Cold Fruit Soup

1 qt. dark red or black cherries
1 small bottle of claret (red wine)
1 stick cinnamon

1 T. dark brown sugar
1/2 c. cornstarch
1/2 large lemon, sliced

At home, wash, dry, and pit cherries. Bag in a zippered vegetable bag. Pack lemon whole until ready to use. Bag remaining ingredients separately.

In the field, place cherries, wine, twice as much water as there is wine, brown sugar, and cinnamon stick in medium covered saucepan. Heat slowly over medium heat, stirring occasionally. In a small bowl mix cornstarch and 1/4 c. water with a whisk until thick and smooth. When fruit mixture is hot, slowly whisk cornstarch into fruit. Bring to a boil over medium heat, stirring continuously. Soup should become thick and semigelatinous. If it becomes too thick, thin with a little more wine or water. Boil for 1 minute. Remove from heat and pour into a plastic container. When cool, seal with a tight-fitting lid and place in the ice chest. (The lemon slices are for a garnish and should not be added until serving.) AS AN OPTION, prepare soup at home the day before leaving on your trip and refrigerate until ready to pack the ice chest.

DAY THREE MENU

Breakfast

Bam Bam Daybreak

Melon

Coffee and Juice

Lunch

Crowheart Butte Cold Fruit Soup

Whole Wheat Crackers

Root Beer Floats

Dinner

Broadax Beef Olives

High Meadows Salad

Sweet Badlands

Wine, Tea and/or Milk

DAY THREE

Lucky visitors to the canyon during the 1980s through early 2000s were treated to something of a rarity—a chance to see bighorn sheep. A herd of about fifty were reintroduced into the canyon from the Whiskey Mountain Wildlife Habitat near Dubois during the 1980s. One of the last survivors of the Sinks Canyon herd, a ram named Bam Bam, became so acclimatized to humans, he let people get up close and personal with him. He's even starred in a YouTube show charging a truck. Unfortunately, park rangers' efforts to keep him off the road and away from tourists whom he had starting chasing proved less than successful, and Bam Bam had to be relocated to a new home deeper in the Winds.

Instead of bighorn sheep, we get treated to a spectacular display of rock climbing. For obvious reasons, Sinks Canyon draws rock climbers from all over. With difficulties rated from 5.6 through 5.14a, the colorfully named routes such as "Climb Now, Cry Later," "Bust a Nut," and "Searching for Jose Cuervo" test climbers' skills and egos. It's been a while since I climbed the Sandstone Buttress, the first climbable surface inside the park coming in from Lander. It was kind of nice, sitting in my camp chair, drinking good hot coffee and eating breakfast while watching two climbers tackle the multipitch traditional-style climb. I must admit, the part I liked best was rappelling down after the climb. Chuckling to myself, I add more molasses to my Bam Bam Daybreak.

Cane molasses has long been a staple sweetener that added color, taste, and nutrition to foods. However, in the mid-1700s "*West-India* Molasses" became "dear and scarce." A gentleman from Woodstock "purely accidental" discovered a way to make molasses from apples. After grinding and pressing the apples, as for making cider, he reduced the juice by boiling "it in a Copper" for "about 6 Hours gentle Boiling, and by that Time it comes to be of the Sweetness and Consistency of Molasses." Somehow, it didn't catch on.

Day Three Breakfast Recipe

Bam Bam Daybreak

1 lb. pkg. bulk breakfast sausage	**1/4** c. flour
rice, cooked last night after dinner	**1** T. butter
2 eggs	**1/2** c. molasses

Slice sausage into patties and freeze. Bag remaining ingredients separately. Leave melon whole until ready to serve.

In-the-field preparation

Brew coffee. In a medium bowl, mix cooked rice, eggs, butter, and flour until you reach a pastelike consistency. Spread mixture evenly in an oiled baking dish and bake in tailgate oven on 350°F and for 30–45, depending on the altitude at which you are camping. Place sausage patties in large covered skillet and cook over low heat, turning to brown both sides. Cut melon in half, remove seeds, and slice off rind. Serve while the rest of breakfast cooks. When rice cake is done, scoop some on plates, add sausage patties, and drizzle with molasses. Serve. (If you didn't make today's lunch soup last night, prepare it this morning while cooking breakfast.)

THIS MEAL needs no adaptation for a second morning breakfast on a float trip. For all others, cook and dehydrate sausage loose rather than in patties. Cook and dehydrate rice and use powdered eggs.

After we finally pack up and head out of Sinks Canyon, our drive drops us down into the valley that provided some of the best wintering grounds and lots of good sweet water for pronghorns (antelope), moose, deer, bighorn sheep, and buffalo that once inhabited the region. Historians disagree about when English trappers first ventured into the Lander valley, but we do know that trappers decimated the valley's beaver population by 1840. An article in the *Merchant's Magazine and Commercial Review* in 1851 complained that the beaver skin business had shrunk to a twentieth of what it had been in 1839. During the early 1830s, trappers killed at least four million beavers a year to satisfy the demand for hats made from beaver fur. According to Angus Laut, beaver fur "wears like buffalo hide," standing up well to constant use. Better still, "every atom of the beaver was minted into coin or profit." Not only were beaver pelts used in making coats and the fur pounded into felt for hats, "the tail was a great delicacy on the banquet board" while "the general flesh was preferable to game birds." Then there was the castoreum, which sold to the perfume trade for a hefty amount. Mandy murmured something about the essence of beaver likely drove men wild. Linda decided it probably drove them away.

As we pull onto Lander's main street and head for the grocery store to replenish our supply of fresh foods, breads, and ice, Linda asks me why the small town, originally named Pushroot because the plant roots appeared to push their way out of the soil in spring, has a five-lane-wide road plus room for parallel parking on both sides of the street. Simple. Lander was *the* place to go for supply, which meant loads of all sorts of goods arrived in the town via wagons pulled by a jerk line of as many as twenty horses. The buildings were set far enough across from each other to allow the drivers to be able to turn their team of horses and the wagon around in the street. That took a lot of room. When trucks replaced wagons and the road was paved, Lander ended up with a nice wide avenue.

Of course, it was also a road that ultimately gave Lander its current name. In 1859, chief engineer Col. Frederick W. Lander led an expedition that mapped out the Fort Kearney, South Pass, and Honey Lake Wagon Road, better known as the Lander Trail. It went west through the South Pass by the Wind River Range and on to Fort Hall in Idaho. Although the road did not pass through what would become the town, it did open up the area. The town of Lander received official incorporation in 1890.

On a June day in 1910, the school board president sat on his horse on a mountain ridge overlooking the town and contemplated what he would say to the graduating high school class. His surroundings inspired him. Looking at the snowcapped peaks, he decided, "May your ideals and aspirations be as lofty and your purposes as steadfast as are these." Looking out over the broad green and growing valley, he thought, "May your lives be rich and fruitful as are these." Looking at the town nestled so quiet and secure in valley, he wished, "May your way through the world be quiet and peaceful and progressive as this." Looking over the flats and foothills stretching out on all sides around the valley, he hoped, "May the possibilities of life riches in you be presently found and utilized in you, even as are these material riches coming now to be." Good sentiments.

On our way out of town, we pass the site where Camp Augur (later Fort Brown) originally stood. The army established the camp as part of an arrangement made with Shoshone Peace Chief Washakie when the government created the Wind River Indian Reservation for the Shoshone Nation in 1868. It was later moved fifteen miles to present-day Fort Washakie on the reservation, our next stop.

In June 1878, James Brisbin and six friends journeyed from Omaha, Nebraska, to the Wind River country via the South Pass and Lander to hunt and fish. Brisbin came up the valley along a path that would become the road we travel. This is how he described the scene that met him: "Our journey now lay through a series of ridges and sandhills covered with sage-brush; and after riding fifteen miles we climbed a steep hill, and the Great Wind River Valley lay before us. The river wound like a band of silver among the trees, and its banks were dotted with herds of horses and cattle. An immense Indian village stretched for a mile on the green sod, and hundreds of dogs and children frolicked before the lodges. At the head of the valley were the agency buildings, and beyond stood Fort Brown."

The Wind River Indian Reservation was originally set aside for the Shoshones and the Bannocks; however, the latter received their own reservation in Idaho. The Arapaho, traditional enemies of the Shoshones, were to receive their own reservation in Colorado; however, the U.S. government asked the Shoshones if the Arapahos could spend one winter on the Shoshones' reservation. That was 1877. These two nations have shared the same reservation ever since. Each nation has its own government, headquartered in Fort Washakie, named in honor of Chief Washakie. He became a principal chief of the Shoshone Nation in 1840 and maintained strong, peaceful ties with the Americans. He, along with eight hundred Shoshones, met with Colonel. Lander near the South Pass on July 3, 1859. The Office of Indian Affairs had sent four wagons west with Lander loaded with $5,000 worth of goods, including cooking utensils, clothing, and blankets, to distribute to Chief Washakie and his people as a goodwill gesture. The U.S. government needed the Shoshones' continued peaceful relations to help keep the Oregon Trail and cutoffs such as Lander's that crossed through the Shoshones' lands safe for travelers. Famed Western artist Albert Bierstadt, a member of Lander's expedition, wrote, "It was very picturesque to see them coming across the plain with hundreds of horses, all packed with their dwellings and all they possessed. Their lodge poles are packed on each side of the horses with one end resting on the ground, and across them they rig a seat which they call a buggy; it will accommodate two persons. In about an hour after their arrival their lodges were all set up, and their families seated inside. An ox was slaughtered and they had a grand feast."

We stop at the general store for some cold root beer and ice cream to make floats to go with our lunch, which we plan to eat at the State-run rest area up the highway from Fort Washakie. The open vistas with the Winds for a backdrop and the patches of cottonwoods shading the banks of the Wind River appear as idyllic spots for a picnic, however, the reservation is not public land. It is sovereign land belonging to the Shoshones and Arapahos.

The picnic area at the rest stop, nestled in the curve of the highway, supplies a panoramic view of the Winds behind and a sweeping valley settled against the buttes. The first order of business is making root beer floats. Root beer really started out as a form of beer made from roots. A "farmer's wife" submitted her root beer recipe to *The American Farmer and Rural Register* in 1871. She said to "take a quantity of sarsaparilla roots and sassafras bark and some hops and boil till the strength is extracted. To three gallons of the liquor, after it is strained, add one quart of molasses and a cup of yeast. After standing in a warm place eight or ten hours, strain again and bottle. It will be fit for use the following day."

Day Three Lunch Recipe

Crowheart Butte Cold Fruit Soup (see above)

Root Beer Floats

1 liter bottle root beer   **1** qt. vanilla ice cream

Pack the plastic bottle of root beer. Purchase the ice cream on the trip.

In-the-field preparation

Divide soup between the bowls. Slice lemon and place slices on top of soup. Serve with crackers. Divide ice cream evenly between mugs or plastic glasses. Add root beer. Serve.
    THIS MEAL *doesn't work for other kinds of trips. Choose another.*

In 1833, Captain Benjamin Bonneville (whom the salt flats in Utah were named) headed an expedition through this region. Four years later, Washington Irving wrote an account of Bonneville's journey in *The Rocky Mountains, or Scenes, Incidents and Adventures in the Far West*. Spreading out from the base of the mountains, Irving described "a confusion of hills and cliffs of red sandstone, some peaked and angular, some round, some broken into crags and precipices, and piled up in fantastic masses; but naked and sterile. There appeared to be no solid favorable to vegetation, nothing but coarse gravel; yet, this isolated barren landscape was diffused with such atmospherical tints and hues, as to blend the whole into harmony and beauty." Bonneville's party, skirting along the Wind River through groves of willows and cottonwoods and grassy meadows made their way up the valley to the vicinity of present-day Fort Washakie. Late in the afternoon, Bonneville spotted smoke in the distance among the hills ahead. Fearing that it came from the campfire of "some hostile band," he and one other advanced to investigate. What they found was not campfire smoke, but vapors rising from "hot springs of considerable magnitude, pouring forth steams in every direction over a bottom of white clay. One of the springs was about 25 yards in diameter, and so deep, that the water was of a bright green color." Brisbin also bathed in the hot sulphur springs, writing that they "cover hundreds of acres, and are from three to one hundred feet deep. The water is of a dark-blue color and strongly

impregnated with sulphur. The flow from them is grand, forming, where it empties into the Wind River, a creek over twenty feet wide." Evidently it was popular with diving duck, too. Brisbin said that several were swimming about "quite complacently, and apparently enjoying their warm bath as much as we did."

The hot springs are located a few miles southeast of us. They are a great place to sit and soak in a private bath or play in a geothermal heated pool. They also represent one of the compromises we made in planning our "good health, and real joy-producing recreation . . . motor camping game" as dubbed by Howard Slaten in 1926, when auto tours became an "a national institution, and America's favorite pastime." We could spend the entire week exploring the areas around any one of the locations on our itinerary. Mandy, Linda, and Connor made hard choices in whittling down their wish lists into a manageable trip that accommodated the key things they each wanted to see and do. As for me, I was thrilled to get to spend time with a dear friend and play tour guide, one of my favorite hobbies.

After lunch, Connor can't wait to get a better look at Crowheart Butte just up the road a few miles. This lone butte, near the small town of Crowheart, comes into view quite a distance before we pull into the scenic turnout opposite the butte for better viewing. Linda asks if the legend about the butte's name is true. As the story goes, the claystone and sandstone formation received its name from a battle fought in 1866 between the Shoshones and the Crows over the rights to the rich hunting grounds found in the Wind River Basin. Neither side appeared to gain the upper hand, so Chief Washakie and Crow Chief Big Robber decided to meet in hand-to-hand combat to the death to determine the victor of the war. After fierce fighting, Washakie defeated Big Robber. The victory celebration took place on top of the butte where, as the legend goes, Washakie cut out Big Robber's heart and ate it. Chief Washakie who lived well into his nineties and passed away in February 1900, neither confirmed nor denied the story when interviewed by reporters.

Back in the car, we make tracks for Dubois, pronounced DŪ-boys. Early white settlement began around the late 1800s. The place quickly took on a rather unattractive reputation as home to working men who didn't seem to work hard enough to break a sweat. The town was dubbed "Never Sweat," a name the U.S. Postal Service refused to use when they put in an office. The postal service picked the name "Dubois" in honor of an Idaho senator of the time who was very generous and diligent in acquiring funding for the postal department.

Intriguing badlands meet the town on the east. Variegated red and gray bands of prehistoric lake and stream sediments characterize this natural wonder. Turning onto Horse Creek Road, known locally as the dump road for obvious reasons, we pass the sanitary landfill and enter the unique topography of the Dubois Badlands Wilderness Study Area, situated on 4,520 acres in the Bureau of Land Management system. We stop by the trail kiosk for the two-mile-long interpretive trail that leads into Mason Draw and wander around. (Not hiking the trail was another of the compromises.) Still, everyone's camera gets a workout, especially when Mandy spots a mature bald eagle gliding silently overhead, keeping an eye out for his lunch. The badlands, a series of more or less flat-topped benches and eroded drainages look surreal in the afternoon sun. Bands of sedimentary rock and clays present a striking array of striated colors from a deep red to orange, to amazing lavender and pink, to tan, cream, and gray, with sagebrush dotting the lower slopes and on the upper slopes a scattering of limber pines adding shades of green to this artistic palette. Here and there the claystone has worn away, leaving pinnacles or spires rising up as sentinels. Linda gets so excited when a couple of mule deer wander into view, stopping to browse on some vegetation growing along the ridge top. A few minutes later, we hear a couple of cars crunching up the dirt road and by mutual consent we pile back into the car and head for the Scenic Overlook.

The improved gravel road winds sharply uphill about a mile. The first thing we see is the stunning spire of ancient volcanic sediment, known as Ramshorn Peak. It soars 11,635 feet into the sky and the DuNoir Valley. But that's just the start. To the south and west, we see the full force of the Wind River Range and Whiskey Mountain, home to the United States' largest wintering grounds of Rocky Mountain bighorn sheep; to the north the Absaroka Mountains, pronounced ăb-SŌR-kă, dominate; and to the east, the badlands for the visual feast of a real IMAX experience—360 degrees of panoramic vistas. Connor points to the DuNoir and the Wind River valley spread out below and tells us of the clash between the glaciations Titans. Evidently, the Du Noir glacier thrust into the Wind River valley and effectively blocked off the Wind River glacier. The Du Noir also dumped heaps of moraine two miles into the Wind

River valley through which the river flows today; however, the moraine forced the river toward the southwestern slope of the mountain valley where it cut through the a portion of Tensleep Sandstone that ultimately formed the narrow gap, with some impressive-looking walls through which the highway run between Dubois and Grand Teton National Park.

About six miles northwest of town on our way to the Tetons, we stop at the Tie Hack Memorial. Timber harvesting became a major part of Dubois's industry and income around the turn of the twentieth century when Scandinavian settlers came to Dubois, becoming the "knights with broadaxes" who cut ties for the Chicago and Northwestern Railroad from 1914 until the early 1950s. In 1905, an anonymous author described the art of tie hacking. Once the lumberjack felled several trees, the hacker hewed them with his broadax, a formidable affair having a blade from ten to sixteen inches in length, and weighing from six to twelve pounds. Yet, in spite of the cumbersomeness of this tool, the hacker handles it with a skill and accuracy truly marvelous. Without line or rule he guides the keen blade in smooth and even course along the trunk, relying entirely on his "mechanical eye," as he terms his careful perceptive judgment and control in wielding the ax. Mounting the log and moving backward step by step, timing his progress in careful sequence with the delivery of each stroke, he swings the ax far back over his shoulder, then fetches it forward and down with a ringing stroke that cleaves cleanly through the soft pine, and sending a cascade of fragment chips pattering about. Thus stroke by stroke the scored sides are hewed to the ringing rhythm of the "broadax." Then the hacker cuts the trunk into regular eight-foot tie-lengths, peels the bark from the unhewn sides, puts his 'cut' or 'brand' on each section, and those ties are made.

When the Wind River swelled with spring melt, the tie hackers would float the heavy ties out of the mountains via an elaborate flume. The logs would enter the Wind River and continue their journey downstream to Riverton eighty miles away. During the peak year of 1947, tie hackers' broadaxes cut seven hundred thousand hand-hewed railroad ties.

Our drive then winds past the Pinnacle Buttes and up through mountain conifers and the stunning rock cliffs. Off to the left down in some willows, Linda spots a bull moose browsing on the new growth. I slow down, but there's no place to turn off for a better look. I assure them we'll find a nice viewing stop up on top of Togwotee Pass, pronounced TŌE gŭh tēē. At an elevation of 9,658 feet, it crests the Continental Divide. Supposedly, in 1873, Engineer Corps surveyor Captain William A. Jones named the mountain pass in honor of their Dukurkani guide, Togwetee. Historians called the Dukurkani, a branch of the Shoshones, Sheepeaters because they were skilled hunters of bighorn sheep. Unfortunately, Jones mispronounced and thus misspelled Togwetee's name, and it became Togwotee on the maps. I qualify this with supposedly because some accounts say Togwotee was Shoshone rather than Dukurkani, and there is some debate over the meaning of his name as well. According to Jones, the name meant Lance Striker. Others have translated Togwotee as spear or lance thrower or "goes [or sees] from this place" or "shoots with a spear [arrow or gun]." Around 1900, the Army Corps of Engineers constructed a military road linking Fort Washakie with Fort Yellowstone in what's the national park today. The road followed Jones's route over Togwotee Pass.

I pull into the promised turnout so we can breathe in the crisp, pine-scented air whispering through the trees. Blackrock Creek winds through open meadows that are great fun to cross-country ski or snowshoe through a good part of the year. Stewart not so jokingly wrote to her friend that Wyoming had three seasons, "winter, July, and August." It's June and there are tempting patches of snow. Connor and Linda race to them and attempt to make snowballs. They won't hold together well, so by the time Mandy and I join in, we're all throwing loose snow at each other. The mountain meadows that stretch between the road and the foothills have been described as "natural parks." We were hoping to catch a glimpse of a black bear munching on chokecherries and serviceberries that spring up along the creeks or a moose grazing amid the willows that thrive in the marshy ground beside the stream that weave circuitous routes through valley or maybe an elk mother and her young grazing. No such luck today, probably because we're making too much noise laughing.

But the day grows late. After shaking the snow out of our clothes, we again hit the road. This time to our final destination for the day, our reserved spot at a campground near Moran Junction where the highway Ys to Yellowstone or Grand Teton National Park. Although indirectly named for Thomas Moran, an illustrator who accompanied Ferdinand V. Hayden's 1871 expedition into Yellowstone, the junction obtained its name from the mountain, Mount Moran, in the Teton Range. The expedition named the peak after the artist. All the campgrounds in Grand Teton National Park subscribe to the first-come-first-get system, and when planning the trip, we knew we'd be way too late to get a spot in the park.

Tonight's dinner take little time to throw together, and the dessert includes two of Mandy's favorites, blueberries and graham crackers. From about 1830, whole wheat was often called Graham flour (and yes, Graham crackers because they are made with whole wheat flour) after a healthy food advocate named Sylvester Graham. He insightfully believed that common health issues of the day were related to diet, and removing bran from flour and refining it into white flour lessened the nutritional value. Graham crusaded for health laws and published *The Graham Journal of Health and Longevity*. Devoted to the practical illustration of the science of human life, as taught by Sylvester Graham and others between 1837 and 1839, publishing "recipes for cooking every variety of food in the best manner possible, as fast as those ladies who have tried experiments will furnish us the means."

Day Three Dinner Recipes

Broadax Beef Olives

4 slices roast beef, 1/4 inch thick
1 small onion
1 2.25 oz. can of sliced or minced black olive
1/2 c. red bell pepper, finely chopped
1/2 c. green bell pepper, finely chopped
1/2 c. celery

1 c. Italian bread crumbs
1 egg
2 T. oil
1 1.2 oz. pkg. Béarnaise sauce
1 c. milk
1/4 c. butter
4 toothpicks

Freeze roast beef with pieces of deli paper between them. Wash and dry vegetables, but leave whole until ready to use. Pack remaining ingredients separately.

160

High Meadows Salad

1 small bunch buttercrunch lettuce   **6** radishes
1 small yellow summer squash   **1/4** c. wine vinegar
4 green onions

Wash and dry vegetables. Bag separately in zippered vegetable bags. Refrigerate until ready to leave. Pack in ice chest. Pack vinegar.

Sweet Badlands

8 graham crackers   **1** pt. fresh blueberries
1 qt. fresh strawberries   **1/2** c. sour cream

Wash and dry berries. Pack in vegetable zipper bags. Pack whole crackers separately. Pack sour cream in ice chest when ready to leave.

In-the-field preparation

Finely chop onion, peppers, and celery and set aside. Drain olives. One at a time, place slices of beef on cutting board and place 1/4 of each vegetable on the slice of beef. Keep mixture 1/2 inch from ends. Roll up and pin closed with a toothpick. Repeat until all four have been prepared. Whisk egg in a medium bowl. Pour bread crumbs into a plate. Dip beef roll into egg and then roll in bread crumbs. Sauté in a large covered skilled with oil on medium heat until tender and brown, turning once. You may need to add a little water about halfway through cooking. Shred lettuce into individual bowls. Slice remaining vegetables and distribute evenly among the bowls. Drizzle with wine vinegar. Prepare Béarnaise sauce with milk and butter in a small saucepan according to the direction on the package. Place beef olive on plate. Pour sauce over it. Serve with salad and wine and/or tea. For dessert, mash berries while still in their individual bags. In individual bowls, layer a cracker, 1/4 of the blueberries, a cracker, 1/4 of the strawberries. Top with a dollop of sour cream. (Yes, sour cream!) Serve.

THIS MEAL can be prepared as is for a first night float trip. For all others, dehydrate roast beef in thin strips. Dehydrate the other vegetables and fruits for dessert. Use powdered egg and replace sour cream with powdered milk. Choose another vegetable recipe to replace the salad.

SPECIAL: As we have someplace to be before daybreak, I set up a wee hours of the morning snack to hold us until we can have a late morning breakfast. While a fresh pot of coffee brews, I slice 4 slices of cheese and lay it on 4 pieces of sour dough bread and place in the tailgate oven. I also fill a saucepan with 4 c. apple cranberry juice and add 1 t. of cinnamon and cover it.

DAY FOUR MENU

Breakfast

Ballooning Breakfast
Sour Dough Toast
Yogurt
Coffee and Juice

Lunch

Saddle and Rider Sandwiches
Apricots
Limeade

Dinner

Blacktail
Homestead
Pronghorns
Tea and/or Milk

DAY FOUR

Excitement sparks like electricity through camp this morning even though we're up well before dawn. The still air holds its breath, not even sighing at the sight of the stars. With no lights around to dim the stars and a thin atmosphere between us and them, the stars flicker like tiny, far-off campfires. Today is not one of the area's sixty frost-free days per annum. It coats every surface and forces me to put on my gloves. Cold nips my nose as I heat coffee for Mandy and me and turn apple cranberry juice into a hot drink with a dash of cinnamon for Linda and Connor. In the camp oven, cheese melts on sourdough toast. One farmwife called sourdough starter "witch yeast" which she made from some yeast, lard, sugar, and flour. The snack will tide us over until after our dawn adventure.

When we arrive at our launch point, our pilot, Tony, is busy filling the balloon with hot air. Chatting with Brian and Georgianna, the couple also going up, we learn this balloon ride represents an achievement of a long-held goal for them as well, wrapped up in the form of a thirty-fifth wedding anniversary celebration. They've never been to Wyoming and are hoping to see lots of wildlife. Brian can't get over how cold it is in the morning. A humorist early in the 1900s claimed Wyoming had but two seasons, winter and Fourth of July. When I told them this, Georgianna decides he must have been describing Jackson Hole.

Tony ushers all of us into the gondola, and off we go! No sensation of movement accompanies liftoff. It almost feels like we're standing still and the scenery passes by. And the quiet is incredible. We can hear animals rustling around on the ground below us. Tony explains air current patterns in the Jackson Hole valley. They resemble one-way streets at different elevations. We ascend to one level to allow the gentle winds on the lee side of the Tetons to nudge us in the direction of town and shift to another height to head toward the mountains, making it a round trip rather than unidirectional.

Sunrise splashes golden light over the mountains as the balloon rises up from the valley floor like the Tetons themselves. Rising one and a half miles almost perpendicular from the valley, with no foothills to allow the eye to adjust via a gradual ascent, the full force of the eleven- to thirteen-thousand-plus peaks hits you unadulterated. Connor informs everyone that the Tetons are formed out of very old rock even though they are the newest range in the country, thrusting onto the scene approximately nine million years ago. That sounds old, until you compare it with the neighboring Winds at approximately sixty million years. Geologists estimate the granite and gneiss to comprise

the core of the Tetons to be around three billion years old. The product of a geological fault, the Teton Range continues to rise while the Jackson Hole valley drops. Georgianna blushes when Connor blurts out that French *voyageurs*, who were so love-starved by the time they reached the range, they longingly named the three prominent peaks of Grand, Middle, and South Teton *les trios tetons*, the three breasts. Mandy bites back a laugh, but there is a lovely irony in calling a national park the Grand Breast. I plan to remind Connor of this crack when we explore the area's "bosom politics" tomorrow. For the moment, however, I jump in, explaining how Nathaniel Langford, one of early climbers to summit Grand Teton, suggested the name constituted a misnomer. "But 'tis distance that lends enchantment to such a view of these mountains, for when nearly approached, those beautiful curvilinear forms that obtained for them this delicate appellation become harsh and rugged and angular." Langford considered calling them the three Titans "would have better illustrated their relation to the surrounding country." Another expedition member decided the peaks looked more like sharks' teeth than women's breasts.

Federal law prohibits balloons flying into Grand Teton National Park airspace, but from an altitude of over four thousand feet, the jagged snowcapped Tetons take our breath away. While the "caravan encamped three days, to give their animals opportunity to recruit," one traveler in 1838 climbed up to the top of "a very high mountain" to the west of the Tetons. "The prospect was an extensive as the eye could reach, diversified with mountains, hills and plains." Once his gaze fell upon the Tetons, he stood mesmerized. "Here I spent much time in looking over the widely extended and varied scenery, sometimes filled with emotions of the sublime, in beholding the towering mountains—sometimes with pleasure in tracing the windings of the streams in the vale below; and these sensations frequently gave place to astonishment, in viewing the courses in which the rivers flow on their way unobstructed by mountain barriers. After some hours occupied in this excursion, I descended to the encampment, much gratified." Awed by the vistas, we know exactly how this anonymous trekker felt.

Far below, a herd of elk graze in a meadow bordered by "quakies," what locals call quaking aspen trees. Birds call; their voices sing up to us. Moseying above a ribbon of water, Connor spots a bull moose emerging from some willows. His rack of antlers stretches well beyond his body on either side, so wide we wonder how he can lift his head. Beyond, the town of Jackson sits tucked in between the Teton, Wyoming, Gros Ventre (pronounced grōw vŏnt), and Wind River ranges. Ski slopes at both Jackson Hole and Snow King, their upper ends still snow covered, appear to slide down the mountain sides, flanked by pine forests.

Then before we know it, we're touching down gently on the ground again. As a ballooning tradition, our excursion ends with a champagne and juice toast. What a way to start the day!

Back at camp, the newly certified aeronauts compare photos while I get breakfast ready.

Day Four Breakfast Recipe

Ballooning Breakfast

8 eggs	**1/2** green bell pepper
1/2 lb. thick sliced bacon	**1** c. shredded cheese
4 green onions	**1/2** c. milk
1/2 red bell pepper	**3** T. oil

Cook bacon at home by frying, baking, or microwaving. Bag and freeze. Leave vegetables whole until ready to use. Pack eggs, cheese, oil, and milk separately. Pack frozen bacon in the ice chest just before leaving.

In-the-field preparation

Chop onions, peppers, and bacon. Sauté them in a large skillet over medium heat until onions become transparent. Break eggs into a medium bowl; add milk and whisk together until mixed well. Pour egg mixture into skillet over the vegetables. Cover, reduce heat to low, and watch carefully. Do not stir egg vegetable mixture. When the sides of the egg have pulled away from the sides of the skillet, carefully make sure the edges are not sticking to the skillet by running a spatula around the edge. Then begin to carefully lift edges of the omelet with a spatula, eventually loosening the entire omelet. When the top is no longer loose or runny, gently and slowly work spatula under entire omelet. Using the spatula, cut omelet in half, add shredded cheese, and flip the other half over the half with cheese on it and cook for two to three more minutes, allowing cheese to melt. Divide into four wedges. Serve with a cup of yogurt, coffee, and juice.

THIS MEAL can be fixed as is for a first- or second-day breakfast on a float trip. Dehydrate vegetables for a horse or goat trip. Choose another breakfast for a backpacking trip.

Indulging in some of the natural history of the area this morning, Mandy insists the afternoon should take us through some of the Grand Teton National Park's human history. First stop, the Cunninghams' cabin offers a manifestation of the best and the worst of the valley's colorful and, often, notorious human history. Their original cabin stands as a lone guardian of this side of the valley, a short walk from the parking area. Nevertheless, I hand out water bottles and hats. The sun now beams warmly down on us, and although we're in the valley, we're still at an elevation of over six thousand feet.

One of the earliest homesteaders in the valley, John Pierce Cunningham, along with his wife Margaret, established their 160-acre Bar Flying U Ranch on this patch of ground in the shadow of Tetons in 1890. As we approach the structure, the cabin looks like a long rectangular face with a wide uninterrupted brow hanging low over square window eyes and flaring square nostrils. For the first five years, they lived in the two-room "dog trot" style log cabin, the dog trot giving the cabin face its flaring nostril appearance. An architectural form native to the Appalachian mountains of the eastern United States, the dog-trot cabin consists of two small, usually single-room square cabins connected and covered by one gable roof. The open veranda between the rooms where dogs like to lounge, hence the name, offered cool ventilation in summer and could be closed off during Jackson's long, cold winter, making a handy storage space for a plentiful supply of dry firewood. Cunningham's assembly technique required no pegs or hard to come by nails. He cut each log with a "saddle-V" notching system, called a "saddle and rider" corner, so the timbers fit together as tightly as today's prefabricated Lincoln log houses.

Looking out over the grayish-greenish sagebrush, Linda finds it hard to imagine that the land every produced anything, but in the early days, thanks to lots of back-breaking work and irrigation, the Cunninghams raised cattle and hay. At one point their herd reached one hundred head, and they owned eight horses with which the couple farmed. Their one hundred-acre hayfield produced seventy tons of important winter feed for the livestock. Then in 1928, they sold the ranch and moved to Idaho.

The cabin might have fallen into obscurity had it not been for one sensational event that occurred in 1892. The Cunninghams, who spent that winter on another ranch on Flat Creek, let a couple of wranglers named George Spencer and Mike Burnett use the sod-roofed cabin while they pastured a fine-looking herd of horse at the north end of the valley. Come spring, five men snowshoed over Teton Pass, passing themselves off as "deputy sheriffs." They spread rumors that Spencer and Burnett had stolen the horses up in Montana. Enlisting the aid of a few locals, the "posse" headed for the Bar Flying U Ranch. The "deputies," who held no legal jurisdiction in Wyoming (if they actually had any anywhere), lay in wait in the barn until just after daybreak when Spencer appeared to tend to the horses. They ordered the wrangler to surrender. But Spencer, an excellent marksman, pulled out his six-shooter. Unfortunately, the "posse" shot him full of holes before he could do any damage.

Burnett then emerged from the cabin, holding both a rifle and a pistol. He fared no better. The "posse" then buried the wranglers in one unmarked grave in the draw southwest of the Cunningham cabin, and the "deputies" took possession of the herd. Industrious meets infamous! That's Cunningham Cabin. Of course, Cunningham played a small role in the formation of Grand Teton Nation Park as well.

Having seen a bird's eye view of the Tetons, we make our next stop the Snake River Scenic Overlook for a different perspective of the range. The turnout affords a spectacular view up and down the valley of the jutting range. When Langford first encountered the range, he remarked, "Rough, jagged, and pointed, they stood out before us . . . shining like gigantic crystals in the morning sunbeams." Mandy cannot believe that billboards and a clutter of unsightly buildings running along this section of highway once obscured this exquisite natural panorama. Cunningham felt so passionate about the Teton Range, he petitioned the U.S. government in 1925 to preserve it "for the education and enjoyment of the Nation as a whole." Horace Albright, superintendent of Yellowstone National Park at the time, wanted to incorporate the Teton Range under Yellowstone's umbrella. Jackson Hole citizens expressed outrage as they would lose tax revenue, income, grazing rights, and control over the land.

Enter John D. Rockefeller, Jr. He and his family vacationed in Yellowstone during the summer of 1926. Albright personally took Rockefeller on a tour of the Teton valley and lobbied his idea. Taken by the stunning beauty of the mountain, Rockefeller launched the Snake River Land Company and began purchasing ranches and other properties along the Tetons as they were put up on the market for sale. Three years later, Congress passed a bill establishing Grand Teton National Park that consisted of six lakes at the base of the range and the National Forest lands that surrounded the lakes. When Rockefeller announced he was donating to the park the thirty-five thousand acres he had purchased from 320 different landowners, accusations of cheating people out of their property surfaced and resulted in a Senate investigation. They found no wrongdoing. In fact, Rockefeller's land company often paid above market value. Still, led by Wyoming congressional delegation, Congress successfully stopped Rockefeller. So he went around them. He persuaded President Franklin D. Roosevelt to issue an executive order in 1943, creating Jackson Hole National Monument adjacent to the park that included not only Rockefeller's holdings, but over 211,000 acres of National Forest and other government-owned lands. Congress voted to abolish the monument. Roosevelt vetoed the bill. This went on until 1950 when Congress finally caved in and expanded Grand Teton National Park to include the monument.

While Connor pulls out binoculars to examine the small glaciers tucked into alcove on the peaks, Mandy and Linda wander off to the side for a better look at the Snake River. When white men first encountered the Shoshones in this valley, dicey communication skills led to comical misunderstanding and erroneous names based on the fact that different cultures place vastly different meanings on sign language. For instance, American trappers mistook the Shoshones' gesture of what they called themselves, waving a hand in a serpentine motion, to mean "Snake." In reality, the Shoshones portrayed the in-and-out action they used to weave grasses together in the construction of their lodges. Historical records refer to these indigenous people as the "Snake Indians," along with the Snake River. The French trappers, however, called the river like they saw it. They denounced it as *la maudite riviere enragee*, the accursed mad river. Wilson Price Hunt's expedition of 1812 shortened it to the Mad River, an apt description of the river's cascades, whitewater, and falls which made passage difficult at best and disastrous for many a glory seeker. At the mention of whitewater, Mandy pales. Linda sighs contentedly. An excursion down the Mad River's thrill-a-second whitewater had topped her wish list.

As Grand Teton National Park does not take reservations for campground, we amble off the highway and head to the Gros Ventre Campground situated along the Gros Ventre River. The indigenous relatives of the Arapahos who encountered the French trappers call themselves White Clay People. Unfortunately, they suffered from the same sort of miscommunication as the Shoshones. The sign made to signify what the White Clay People called themselves, passing both hands over their stomachs, translated in the French minds as *gros ventre*, "big bellies." Ethnographers catalog Gros Ventre as the *S:ap*, which translated into Paunch.

We lunch amid cottonwoods and spruce trees that hug the riverbanks on one side of us and a two-mile-wide Madison limestone butte on the other that emerges over seven thousand feet out of the glacier carved valley floor. It resembles an oval-shaped bowl that a giant haphazardly dumped upside down. When I pass out our sandwiches, I hand Mandy a bag with a couple of extra onion slices. Onions are one of her favorite foods. In ancient times, in what is now known as the Middle East, the onion bulb grew wild. Cheops, an Egyptian Pharaoh, paid laborers working on the Great Pyramid in onions. The vegetable was so popular that "Egyptian mummies set out for the afterlife with a stock of onions carefully wrapped in bandages." When archaeologists first discovered them in sarcophagi, they mistook them for small mummies.

Day Four Lunch Recipe

Saddle and Rider Sandwiches

2 5 oz. cans white albacore tuna
1 small onion, finely chopped
2 sticks celery, finely chopped
2 T. sweet pickle relish

1 t. ground black pepper
3 T. mayonnaise
   rye bread

> *Wash and dry celery. Pack ingredients separately. Pack 12 apricots. Pack limeade.*

In-the-field preparation

> *Drain tuna, discarding the liquid into a used plastic bag. Flake into a medium bowl with a fork. Chop onion and celery and add to tuna. Add pickle relish, pepper, and mayonnaise. Mix with fork until all ingredients are covered in mayonnaise. Spread on rye bread. Serve with apricots and limeade.*
>
> **AS AN OPTION** *on float, goat, or horse trips, replace mayonnaise with mustard. Choose another sandwich filler for backpacking.*

This is bear country, so we discard our trash, including the plastic bag containing the tuna liquid, in a specially designed trash receptacle at the campground. Then we stow everything back in the car, including the ice chest, and make certain we leave no enticing bits of food around before exploring the valley very appropriately named Antelope Flats. Spread out on the east side of Blacktail Butte not far from our campsite sits the once densely settled strip of land called Mormon Row, now part of Grand Teton National Park. James I. May originally chose a homestead site in the area in 1894, but it took him two years of hard work and saving to accumulate enough resources to move his family to this valley overshadowed by the Tetons. When they moved onto the land during 1896, several other families came with the Mays.

When I turn onto the road frequented by mountain bikers perhaps more than cars, Mandy stares at the perfectly straight road. Locals dubbed it "Mormon Row" for a reason. The followers of the Church of the Latter-day Saints, the Mormons, laid out this mountain valley community in the same orderly fashion as found in Utah and Idaho with homesteads lined up in a straight line. Gazing out over the flatlands awash with sagebrush we see a cluster of bison (buffalo) grazing they way up the quiet valley. Bison had been hunted out in the valley by the time the first homesteaders arrived. Free-ranging bison were accidentally reintroduced to the valley in 1968 when fifteen of these massive creatures broke through the fencing of the Jackson Hole Wildlife Park (now defunct). They made a comfortable home in the vicinity of the Row.

Imagining a busy community comprised of the fifteen homestead claims that originally created Mormon Row, each with 160 acres of land, a house, outbuildings, and tilled soil would require real effort were it not for the Andy Chambers Homestead Historic District. We stop near this last nearly intact example of this homesteading legacy. Chambers built his log home in 1917, near what turned out to be the center of the settlement. He and his brother Jim even constructed the outbuildings—the granary, chicken coop, saddle shed, and machine shed—in a row to the side of the house and barn. A short time later, Andy married Ida Kneedy, the schoolteacher on Mormon Row. While he went off to fight in World War I, Ida proved up on their homestead, plowing by herself forty acres and with the help of neighbors planting them in grain. Upon Andy's return, she drove one team and wagon, he the other, up to Yellowstone where they sold the grain for an unheard-of $5 per one hundred weight. Linda punches her brother in the arm and tells him maybe the range was appropriately named after all because women rule. I add that Ida truly had what the pioneers called "true grit." She continued to make this valley her home even after her parents and youngest brother drowned when the Gros Ventre River flooded.

Across the road from the Chambers homestead sits the Moulton Barn, the most photographed barn in the region that has come to symbolize Jackson Hole. Thomas Alma Moulton and his younger brother John left the family's holdings in Idaho and filed adjoining 160-acre claims on the Row in September 1907. Alma began construction on a barn for his livestock in 1913, a year after he, his wife Lucile, and their infant son settled permanently on the homestead. This barn, with its additions and auxiliary structures, took Alma twenty years to complete. John's barn stands alone down at the end of the row. Of course, we add the famous barns to our photo collections as the sun begins to backlight the Tetons in the background.

Back at the campground, as I toss the andouille in the skillet, I'm thankful for the convenience and innovation in contemporary living. A "farmer's wife" advised women in 1904 to make their own "sausage-meat" "for you are then sure that it will be appetizing, and that the children will thrive upon it." She suggested lean pork, a "saltspoonful of pepper," salt, and sage ground together. Until modern times, cooks encased sausage in the cleaned intestines of the animal from which the meat came.

Day Four Dinner Recipes

Blacktail

1 8 oz. can chicken breast
2 links andouille or hot sausage
1 12 oz. bag veggie spirals pasta
1 29 oz. can chopped tomatoes

4 cloves fresh garlic, chopped
1 2 oz. piece of ginger root, chopped
1 small onion, chopped

Slice sausage, bag and freeze. Leave garlic cloves on the bulb until ready to use. Bag onion and garlic together. Pack remaining ingredients separately.

Homestead

1 cucumber, sliced
2 tomatoes, chopped
1/2 lb. green beans, chopped

2 ears of fresh corn
1/4 c. olive oil
1/4 t. basil

1/4 t. parsley
1/4 t. sea salt

Wash and dry vegetables, except corn. Leave corn in the husk until ready to use. Pack vegetables in separate zippered vegetable bags. Refrigerate until ready to leave on trip.

Pack in ice chest. Mix olive oil, basil, parsley, and sea salt in a plastic bottle.

Pronghorn

2 peaches
4 T. butter, melted
1 c. flour
1/2 c. sugar
1 egg
1 c. milk
2 t. baking powder

Wash and dry peaches. Mix flour, sugar, and baking powder together and bag. Bag remaining ingredients separately.

In-the-field preparation

Sauté sausage in a large skillet over medium heat. Peel garlic, ginger root, and onion. Chop. Add to sausage. Open canned chicken and canned tomatoes and add to sausage, liquid too. (Do not drain chicken or tomatoes first.) Cover and simmer for 20 minutes, stirring occasionally. Meanwhile, fill a large saucepan half full of water and bring to a boil on high heat. Add veggie spirals. Return to a boil. Reduce heat to medium and cook uncovered for 8–10 minutes until done, stirring frequently. While these cook, husk corn and cut off the cob with a knife. (Stand corn up on the stem end on a cutting board. Start at the silk end and slice downward with the knife.). Place in a medium-size bowl. Cut the ends off the green beans and discard. Chop beans, cucumber, and tomatoes. Add to corn. Drizzle with olive oil mixture and toss. When spirals are done, drain and discard liquid. Serve sausage mixture over the spirals and scoop some vegetables beside them on the plate. For dessert, melt butter in a loaf pan in the tailgate oven while preheating it to 350°F. Peel, pit, and slice peaches. Break egg into a small bowl and beat with a whisk. When butter is melted, remove from oven, tilt pan to coat all sides, then pour it into a large bowl containing flour mixture, milk, and egg. Whisk to make a smooth batter. Add sliced peaches. Stir slightly. Pour into loaf pan. Bake for 30–35 minutes. Slice and serve.

THIS MEAL needs no adaptation for a first or second night dinner on a float trip. Cook and dehydrate sausage and chicken, dehydrate vegetables and peaches, and substitute powdered egg and milk for fresh on backpacking, goat, and horse trips.

DAY FIVE MENU

Breakfast

Davey's Hard Boiled Breakfast

Melon

Coffee and Juice

Lunch

Petticoat Pimiento Sandwiches

Corn Chips and Potato Chips

Nectarines

Juice boxes

Dinner

Yellowstone Plateau

Snake River Side

Bear Berries

DAY FIVE

John Colter, a member of the Lewis and Clark Expedition, stopped off in the Jackson area on the return journey, around 1806. He found a profitable "hole," what trappers termed a high mountain valley rich in fur-bearing animals and inhabited by the Dukurkani. Folklore tells of a trapper named Davey Jackson who spent so much time in the valley his partners called the locale Jackson's Hole, although Jackson without the "Hole" didn't become the town's name until it incorporated in 1901.

Mandy and the kids slip into their heavy jackets and hats in the downright cold morning air. The three wander off the get early-morning pictures of the Tetons while I brew coffee and begin cooking our eggs. Preserving this summertime bounty for the wintertime shortage provided much commentary from cooks prior to refrigeration. In 1845, one cook's solution involved plaster of Paris. Although the instruction never mentioned it, I can only assume it remained in powder form rather than being set up with water. In a vessel, the cook poured a layer of plaster in the bottom, then added fresh eggs "being put down as fast as they were laid." They were covered with more plaster, a few inches thick, and "covered the vessel over closely." The trick was getting the eggs to stay "with the small end downward" and not touching each other while being "set in a dry cellar." The cook swore the eggs would be as tasty as newly laid for six months. Another cook swore by using salt rather than plaster of Paris.

Day Five Breakfast Recipe

Davey's Hard-Boiled Breakfast

9 eggs (2 hard-boiled eggs each and 1 for the dumplings)

1 c. milk

1 c flour

1 t. black pepper

Bag flour and pepper together. Pack remaining ingredients separately. Pack melon whole.

In-the-field preparation

Fill a medium saucepan half full of cold water. Gently place 8 eggs in the water. Cover and bring to a boil on high heat. Once eggs are at a full boil, remove from heat and let stand undisturbed for 20 minutes. Meanwhile, in a large covered saucepan, bring 2 qts. of water to a boil over high heat. Beat 1 egg in a medium bowl with a whisk. Add milk and flour mixture. Dough should be sticky but firm. (Add more flour if needed. If too thick,

add a little water). Drop dough into the large pan of boiling water a spoonful at a time.
Cook 6 to 8 at a time for 5–8 minutes (depending on size of dough ball and altitude).
Cut melon, removing seeds and outer rind. Slice. Serve while eggs and dumplings cook.
Remove dumplings from water with a slotted spoon when done and drain on paper towels.
Repeat until all dough has been cooked. Peel eggs and serve with dumplings. NOTE: Use
the water you boiled the eggs in for the dishes.

> ***AS AN OPTION*** *on float trips, substitute powdered milk and prepare no later than*
> *the third day. This could be a first day breakfast option on goat and horse trips. Choose*
> *another breakfast option for backpacking.*

On the way into Jackson, we pass the National Elk Refuge. The Shawnees call
the North American elk wapiti, pronounced WHĀ-pă-tēē. It means "white rump."
Homesteaders settling in the Hole cut the elk off from their winter food supplies
in the valley and they starved by the thousands. Photographer Stephen Leek drew
national attention to their plight in the early 1900s, launching a conservation movement that resulted in the formation of the refuge in 1912. As many as twelve thousand free-ranging elk winter on the refuge. It is an impressive sight!

Entering Jackson, the ski slope that seems to end right at town, which it basi-
cally does, immediately draws the eye. People ski on their lunch hour around here in
winter. The second thing Mandy and the kids notice is that Jackson was built around
a town square, a park. At each corner of it stands an arch constructed of shed elk
antlers collected in the refuge. Encircling the square, under the touristy look lurks
an authentic western town, complete with board sidewalks first installed by the "petticoat government" as newspapers heralded the 1920 election of the first all-woman
town council, including the mayor, in the United States. At the time, the town held
the reputation of being an "outlaw haven" as the town sat seventy-five miles from the
nearest railroad, and winter clogged the mountain passes with enough snow to make
it virtually impossible to get into or out of Jackson Hole for months. With citizens
fed up with an ineffectual town government, the men challenged the women to "do
a better job of getting things done" as Pearl Williams put it. Voters elected them by a
two-to-one margin. One woman even beat out her husband, the incumbent. Mayor
Grace Miller, her all-woman town council, and their appointed marshal, Pearl Williams, initiated a plan to collect long-overdue debts owed to the town, which netted
the coffers $2,000 in two weeks. With the funds, they implemented construction of
culverts over ditches in the roads, purchased the land on which the cemetery rested
that could have been claimed on at any time by anyone so inclined, established a permanent town dump site, had the streets graded, got pools of stagnant water drained
off, and built the first board sidewalks, a feature retained by the current downtown

area. Connor pulls a wry face when I tell them, the ladies of "bosom politics" won reelection by a three-to-one margin.

While in Jackson, we stop at the grocery store and restock the ice chest and foods for the rest of the trip. Then we do our "nooning" as the pioneers use to call lunch in the park. Linda likes corn chips. Connor likes potato chips, so I serve both. What cookbooks called potato chips in the 1880s did not always resemble modern ones. One recipe instructed cooks to peel the potato like removing the peel on an apple, creating long thin ribbons of potato "as long as possible." The ribbons were dried well with a cloth before dropping them into "boiling hot lard." Once golden brown, the cook removed the chips, drained "them well in front of a fire and sprinkled salt and parsley on them."

Day Five Lunch Recipe

Petticoat Pimiento Sandwiches

1 lb. sliced pimiento loaf   whole wheat bread
1/2 lb. sliced swiss cheese   **4** T. mayonnaise

> *Pack all ingredients separately. Pack a bag of corn chips and potato chips, 4 nectarines, and juice.*

In-the-field preparation

> *Spread mayonnaise on bread. Divide pimiento loaf and cheese between the sandwiches. Serve with corn chips, nectarines, and juice.*
>
> ***AS AN OPTION*** *on horse, float, or goat trips, freeze pimiento loaf, replace mayonnaise with mustard, and eat sandwiches for the first or second day lunch. Also suitable for a first day lunch on a backpacking trip.*

Grand Teton National Park beckons again. Entering from Moose, we park in the lot by the Chapel of the Transfiguration, constructed on the bank of the Snake River to serve the employees and guests of outlying dude ranches in the early 1900s. Across from it sits the Menor's Ferry Historic District.

Around 1894, Bill Menor saw an opportunity. No reliable means of transportation existed across the very unreliable Snake River, which divided the Jackson Hole valley. Most of the residents lived on the east bank while the best access to timber, hunting, and the ever-delicious wild huckleberries free for the picking were on the west side. We tour through Menor's cabin and the general store, a key to the community's survival. Struthers Burt, who established one of the area's early dude ranches, described one winter where the passes became so impassable not even the transport wagons on skis could get through. First the general store ran out of the essentials such as flour, sugar, and canned milk. Then all that was left was coffee, dried beans, a few root crops, and canned fruit. Burt complained, "Eventually it became difficult to look a canned peach or a bean or a carrot in the face. And the fact that canned peaches are ordinarily the most expensive of luxuries did not increase the doctor's [his partner] or my appetite for them."

Linda urges us out of the general store. They're boarding the replica of Menor's ferry, and she wants to be able to say she at least boated on the Snake River. We scramble on board and off we go across the river. Menor's ferry did a booming business, especially during times of high water. He used a cable system to pilot his ferry. When he turned the pilot wheel, the cable tightened up, which aimed the pontoons toward the distant bank. Water current pushing against the pontoons literally shoved the ferry across the river. The ferry's design, something along the lines of a catamaran without a sail, allowed Menor to carry a four-horse team and a wagon fully loaded with logs, and later a motorized coach full of dudes headed to one of the ranches in the area. A wagon and team cost its owner fifty cents per ride, while a horse and rider shelled out twenty-five cents. Pedestrians could cross for free, provided Menor happened to be ferrying over a wagon at the same time. By 1918, Menor grew tired of the business and sold his squatted-on homestead (no claim ever showed up under Menor's name) to Maud Noble and her partner Frederick Sandell, who doubled the rates and operated the ferry until 1927 when the Bureau of Public Roads built a steel truss bridge just below the ferry crossing, effectively putting it out of business.

Futzing around puts us a bit behind, which means fewer stops at the scenic turnouts on the drive through the park. The Teton Park Road skirts the base of the range. We'd hardly travel a couple of miles when a thunderstorm pops up; nothing uncommon in this region for this time of year. Naturalist and geologist Fritiof Fryxell even noted them when he characterized the view. "Over these seemingly changeless mountains, in endless succession, move the ephemeral colors of dawn and sunset and of noon and night, the shadows and sunlight, the garlands of clouds with which storms adorn the peaks, the misty rain-curtains of afternoon showers." The shower passes by and clears out by the time we reach the upper end of Jenny Lake, named after Beaver Dick Leigh's Shoshone wife. He, after whom Leigh Lake just up from Jenny Lake is named, guided many an expedition through the hole and beyond, most notable the 1872 Hayden Survey of Yellowstone. A true frontiersman, Leigh hated the ever-encroaching "civilization" and tried to keep at least some wilderness between it and his family. They camped in the Tetons during the three to four months of summer and wintered "at the elbo of the teton [river]" as Leigh called it. Tragedy struck

the family four years after the Hayden expedition. While traveling to their winter cabin, the Leighs came across a trapper and his family infected with smallpox. As Christmas neared, the entire family became sick, one by one. Jenny, soon after giving birth to their fifth child, succumbed to the disease. Ill himself, Beaver Dick watched each of his other children die within eleven days of his wife. He buried his family by the junction of the Teton River.

Connor sighs. He would have liked to have taken the shuttle boat across Jenny Lake and hiked into Cascade Canyon, a deep U-shaped gorge sculpted by glacial flow. Or at least up to Hidden Falls. Instead, we content ourselves watching a bald eagle fish the waters for a meal before rejoining the main highway east of Jackson Lake that takes us into Yellowstone National Park.

Geologists believe volcanic eruptions began occurring in the region of the park 2.5 millions years ago, creating the Yellowstone Plateau. Eruptions persisted until about 70,000 years ago, producing a series of volcanic craters known as calderas. Indigenous peoples hunted and fished the area for over 11,000 years. Their descendants described the extraordinary marvels to members of the Lewis and Clark Expedition, who chalked it up to superstitious nonsense. As we set up camp on the edge of the West Thumb of Yellowstone Lake, I keep thinking about Yellowstone cutthroat trout and wishing I'd brought my fishing pole. There's nothing quite like fresh-caught trout for breakfast side-dressed with a little lemon mayonnaise. During the 1800s mayonnaise-based sauces accompanied a wide variety of dishes, but making it was an art. One New York restaurateur, badgered about his secret recipe, finally confided, "The trouble is wis ze ladies, zat dey do nout knee die salad cold enough in ze preparation. To make ze dressing properly it should be made in ze bowl standing in a dish of cracked ice. Zs lady let ze oil get warm in ze making, and dat make ze dressing oily. Perfect cole is ze secret of mayking mayonnaise."

Day Five Dinner Recipes

Yellowstone Plateau

1 lb. deli sliced ham
1 bunch fresh broccoli
3 T. balsamic vinegar

1 1.2 oz. pkg. hollandaise sauce
4 T. butter
1 c. milk

Freeze ham. Wash and dry broccoli. Remove tough stems ends. Discard. Cut broccoli into bite-sized pieces. Bag in zippered vegetable bag. Bag remaining ingredients separately.

Snake River Side

8 ears corn   **4** T. butter
1 T. plus 1 t. garlic powder   **1** t. mace

Bag ingredients separately. Don't husk corn until ready to use.

Bear Berries

2 bunches seedless grapes   **1/2** c. almond slivers
1 green apple   **1/4** c. mayonnaise
1/2 c. chopped dates   **2** T. lemon juice

Wash and dry grapes and apple. Remove grapes from stems and bag in gallon-size zipper vegetable bag. Mix dates and almonds together. Apple can be stored with other fruit for the trip. Store mayonnaise and lemon juice separately. Pack them in ice chest just before leaving.

In-the-field preparation

Fill large saucepan half full of water. Add 1 T. garlic powder. Cover. Bring to a boil on high heat. Husk corn. Drop ears in boiling water and remove pan from heat. Meanwhile, pour 1 c. water and the vinegar into a medium saucepan. Add the steamer basket filled with broccoli. Cover and bring to a boil over medium heat. When it begins to steam, remove from heat. Prepare hollandaise sauce with milk and butter according to the directions on the package. Arrange ham slices on individual plates. Place broccoli on ham and top with hollandaise sauce. Melt butter, 1 t. garlic powder, and mace in a small saucepan over low heat. Drain corn on paper towels for a few seconds. Place ears on plates and drizzle with butter mixture. Serve. For dessert, core and slice apple. Dip them immediately in the lemon juice, then add slices and the date/nut mix to bag of grapes. Add mayonnaise and mix, turning resealed bag end over end several times. Serve in individual bowls.

THIS MEAL needs no adaptation for a first or second day dinner on a float trip. For all other types of trips, substitute powdered milk and dehydrated ham and vegetables for main course and side and raisins for grapes in the dessert. Do not add mayonnaise.

SPECIAL: For tomorrow's dinner, bring 1 c. rice and 1 1/2 c. water to a boil in a medium covered saucepan over high head. Once it starts boiling, add 1/3 c. more cold water. Simmer 30–40 minutes (possibly longer at high altitude). Rice should be slightly on the mushy side. When cool, bag in a clean plastic bag and store in the ice chest.

DAY SIX MENU

Breakfast

Paint Pots

Melon

Coffee and Juice

Lunch

Upper Falls Salad

Rye Crackers

Kiwis

Buttermilk

Dinner

Wapiti Wraps

Steaming Geyser

Mud Volcano Hasty-Pudding

Tea and/or Milk

DAY SIX

Hayden headed a group of thirty-four men on the U.S. government survey of the Yellowstone country in 1871. His detailed reports, William Henry Jackson's photographs, and Thomas Moran's paintings resulted in Congress establishing Yellowstone as the country's first national park in March 1872. But Henry Washburn's 1870 exploration that was reported by Langford (who then joined Hayden's more comprehensive survey in 1872), in *Scribner's Monthly* stole a bit of Hayden's initial thunder. Ironically, the job of taking some very crude and hastily drawn sketches, the only ones made on the Washburn trip, fell to *Scribner's* staff artist Thomas Moran. Gee, suppose that's why he joined Hayden's expedition the following year? Unfortunately, the harshness of the terrain caught up with Moran, and when the opportunity arose to leave early with a contingent of the expedition's military escort that had been recalled, he took it.

Langford noted that the Washburn party packed in bacon, flour, dried fruits, and other food basics on twelve broncos that often had problems negotiating all the fallen timber and thick forest as the party followed "the slight Indian trail" that was "narrow, rocky, and uneven, frequently leading over high hills, in ascent and descent more or less abrupt and difficult" in the "increasing altitude of the route." Hunters in the group augmented the food stores with pronghorns, rabbits, grouse, ducks, and lots of trout. Our breakfast fare of corned beef hash runs less exotic, unless you consider what cooks in the early 1900s put beef through on order to "corn" it. They packed salt between layered of the "cheaper cuts of meat" in a barrel. After sitting in a cool spot overnight, they added a sugar, baking soda, and saltpeter brine and covered the meat with a lid weighed down with stones or a piece of iron to keep the meat under the brine. "In case any should project, rust would start and the brine would spoil in a short time." Cookbooks also warned to not use molasses as it tended to ferment the brine.

Day Six Breakfast Recipe

Paint Pots

1 15 oz. can corned beef hash   **2** T. oil
8 eggs

> *Pack ingredients and melon separately.*

In-the-field preparation

Heat oil in a large skillet over medium heat. Add corned beef, stirring occasionally. Cut, seed, and remove rind from melon. Slice and serve with coffee and juice while breakfast cooks. Place two qts. water in large saucepot. Cover and bring to a boil over high heat. Preheat tailgate over to 200°F. Once water reaches full boil, crack eggs one at a time into water (no more than two cooking in the pot at one time). When egg is done, usually two to three minutes, carefully remove with a slotted spoon. Place in a dish and keep warm in tailgate oven while cooking remaining eggs. Serve with corned beef hash, either with egg on top of hash or on the side.

THIS MEAL needs no adaptation for horse, goat, or float trips, provided it is served the first days. Also a first day breakfast for backpacking is you don't mind the extra weight.

SPECIAL: For lunch today, chop all the fresh vegetables for the salad, except bean sprouts. Re-bag together in zippered vegetable bag the lettuce was stored in. Open olives and shrimp and drain. Store the drain juices in a used plastic bag and dispose of it in a bear-save trash container located in the park as soon as possible. Add olives and shrimp to vegetables. Store in the ice chest.

Being "bone biting" chilly this morning, I make extra coffee and some hot tea and load them in the thermoses. Although faced with a steady stream of traffic that, at times seriously, impedes our "junketing-place," the roads make the park's legendary "gigantic pleasure ground" much more accessible than either Langford or Alfred Peale could ever dream possible. In the form of letters posted in the *Philadelphia Press*, Peale reported Hayden's first and most influential trip. He accompanied a small group who spent a week mapping and examining geysers in the basins northwest of Yellowstone Lake. Nobody knows exactly how many geysers erupt in the park; however, we do know that our first stop for the day, the Upper Geyser Basin, holds at least seventy eruptions. That's about a quarter of the world's geysers in one basin. Geologically speaking, Yellowstone remains very active. Peale found it so. Looking down into some of the geyser caverns, he found the water "clear as crystal, the tint seen is a most beautiful blue. I can compare it to nothing but the blue of a clear sky, and even then you must imagine the color intensified. It seems as though the cavity were lined with a portion of the heavens above us, convoluted and rolled over the projecting ridges on the sides of the spring, each one of which throws back the sunlight broken in to its constitute colors."

We move on to Old Faithful, named so by the Washburn party because it erupted right on schedule about every hour for the nine hours they were exploring the area.

Old Faithful's timetable changed about a decade ago due to earthquakes in the basin, lengthening the times between eruptions. Nonetheless, Old Faithful still goes off at predictable times and puts on a show that elicits as much excitement now as the early accounts. Ten years after Hayden, Archibald Geikie retracted much of his predecessor's route. His party arrived at Old Faithful just about the time the undulations began. "The water was surging up and down a short distance below, and when we could not see it for the cloud of vapor its gurgling noise remained distinctly audible. We had not long to wait before the water began to be jerked out in occasional spurts. Then suddenly, with a tremendous roar, a column of mingled water and steam rushed up for 120 feet into the air, falling in a torrent over the mound, the surface of which now steamed with water, while its strange volcanic colors glowed vividly in the sunlight. A copious stream of still steaming water rushed off by the nearest channels to the river." As Old Faithful starts gurgling up water like an irate fountain, the four of us, along with about a hundred others, train our camera on the ephemeral-looking force of nature like paparazzi waiting for the hottest new starlet in Hollywood.

Once the frenzy dies down, we mosey up the road to the Fountain Paint Pots. Here the clay and silica mud pots bubble and boil and spit blobs of mud because they lack enough water to create a geyser. They enthrall Connor as the acids in the water break down the nearby rock, forming the mud, which is colored by the variety of minerals in the rock. Gazing out over them, the pinks, blues, and oranges do resemble containers of paint—messy ones. Were it up to Connor, we'd wander around the area all day. But Linda complains her stomach is growling, so we walk back to the car and locate the nearest picnic area.

Before embarking on their survey mission, Hayden's men partook in a short respite at the Bottler brothers' ranch not far from the present-day park. Peale described it as "the advance guard of civilization," in part because the "hardy mountaineers received us with the most hospitable liberality, their first act being to furnish us with milk *ad libitum* . . . satisfying our thirst for both sweet and butter milk." Buttermilk fortifies our lunch as well. We also dip into the thermoses of hot coffee and tea I made this morning.

Day Six Lunch Recipe

Upper Falls Salad

1 bunch leaf lettuce, shredded
1/2 red bell pepper, chopped
1/2 green bell pepper, chopped
1 small cucumber, sliced
4 large radish, sliced
4 sticks celery, chopped

1 16 oz. pkg. cherry or grape tomatoes
2 carrots, sliced
1 3 oz. pkg. bean sprouts
1/2 Bermuda onion, chopped
1 6 oz.(dry weight) can black olives
1 5 oz. can shrimp

Wash and dry vegetables. Pack separately in zippered vegetable bags. Pack Bermuda onion with other onions and potatoes for the trip. Leave vegetables whole until ready to use. Pack buttermilk in ice chest just before leaving. Pack olives and shrimp with other canned goods. Pack 4 kiwis in ice chest just before leaving.

In-the-field preparation

Divide salad on individual plates. Slice kiwis. Serve salad with rye crackers, kiwis, and buttermilk.

THIS MEAL *needs no adaptation for a first lunch on a float trip; however, it is not suitable for other types of trips. Choose another option.*

Of the 150 waterfalls that grace the park, the falls in the Grand Canyon of the Yellowstone River ranks as the best known, and most certainly among the most spectacular. The river carved the twenty-four-mile-long canyon out of volcanic rock that had been weakened by the acidic gases and hot water from the geyser basin. The canyon's striking colors come from oxides and minerals leaching out of the decaying rocks. Together, the Upper and Lower Falls fall over four hundred feet. When first encountering the canyon, Langford wrote, "The brain reels as we gaze into this profound and solemn solitude." The Yellowstone River flows through a narrowed notch between the rocks. Langford likened its approach to the brink of the upper falls as the water being bound "with impatient struggles for release, leaping through the stony jaws, in a sheet of snow-white foam, over a precipice nearly perpendicular." The river churned over the rocks of the Lower Falls, reducing the water "to a mass of foam and spray, through which all the colors of the solar spectrum are reproduced in astonishing profusion." Washburn's group spent two days rambling around the falls and canyon, reluctantly leaving "with the unpleasant conviction that the greatest wonder of our journey had been seen." As their party did not penetrate as far into the region as Hayden would the following year, for Langford seeing the Grand Canyon of the Yellowstone proved to be the pinnacle of this trip. We agree. As Connor snaps a photo of the falls and canyon, it hits me that we are viewing exactly what Langford saw 140 years ago. And Connor's picture also mirrors one of the sketches that Moran reconstructed to accompany the article. It sends a chill down my spine that has nothing to do with the afternoon cooling off.

Like Langford, we beat a hasty retreat from the "laughing waters" glittering with "rainbows and diamonds" and head for the "snow-crowned peaks" that "glistened like crystal" in the distance. Well, actually, we head for Mud Volcano, but regardless of our direction, we'd be heading toward snow-covered peaks. On their way back to camp after examining some paint pots, Langford hears what Washburn likens to frequent cannon fire. Following the sound the group came across a very active Mud Volcano, spewing steam and clay particles 125 feet high into the surrounding pine trees and scattered it over a 200-foot radius. "Dense volumes of steam shot into the air with each report [the sound of cannon fire], through a crater thirty feet in diameter. The reports, though irregular, occurred as often as every five seconds, and could be distinctly heard half a mile. Each alternate report shook the ground a distance of two hundred yards or more, and the massive jets of vapor which accompanied them burst forth like the smoke of burning gunpowder." Most likely it smelled like gunpowder as well. Too bad Mud Volcano hasn't erupted since 1922. Judging by what we do see, it must have really been something.

On that sad note, we make tracks past the other side of Yellowstone Lake and precede over Sylvan Pass and its dramatic scenic vistas and out of the park via what the locals call the Yellowstone Highway that runs along the North Fork of the Shoshone River through the Wapiti valley. President Teddy Roosevelt pronounced this road "the most scenic fifty-two miles in the US". Most likely this pronouncement came after seeing the strange rock formations with colorful names such as Chinese Wall, the Holy City, and Sleeping Giant. Mandy spots a mountain goat up on top of the wall. We pull over to get a picture. But that's not exactly why famed Buffalo Bill Cody build his Pashaska Tepee guest lodge thirty miles outside the park along this stretch of road. The Crows called Cody Pashaska, which means "long hair." Finished in 1901, Pashaska Tepee and its counterpart the Wapiti Inn, Cody's other strategically place lodge, acted as the only and perfectly timed stage stops between the town and the park.

We set up camp for the night at the campground in the Wapiti valley just beyond Yellowstone. The valley rests in the country's first national forest, the Shoshone. While Mandy and the kids wander over to the Wapiti Ranger Station, the oldest in the nation, built during 1903, I start dinner.

After putting in a long day scrambling to capture Yellowstone's wonders on photographic plates, it thrilled Jackson to see the "white tents of campfire smoke" because they promised a good supper. Mandy, Linda, and Connor settle, instead, for the quiet hiss of the camp stove upon their return. According to a 1915 article in the *Jackson's Hole Courier*, a "camp outfit" cannot be complete without a camp stove. "The convenience and comfort in preparing the meals, the saving of both labor and wood in keeping the pot boiling, and reducing to the minimum the danger of Forest Fires, make it almost indispensable." Single burners cost fifty-five cents in those days and a four burner could be had for $3. Don't I wish!

Day Six Dinner Recipes

Wapiti Wraps

1 5 oz. can chicken breast
1 3.75 oz. can oysters
rice cooked last night (1 c. before
    cooking)
2 T. Parmesan cheese
2 T. butter
1/4 t. nutmeg
1/4 t. mace
1/4 t. parsley

1/2 t. grated lemon peel (lemon zest)
1 4 oz. container light cream
1 egg
1 c. cornmeal
1 c. flour
1/4 c. oil

    Bag Parmesan cheese, nutmeg, and mace together. Grate the peel from 1 lemon and dehydrate. Bag with parsley. Pack remaining ingredients separately.

Steaming Geyser

2 medium green zucchini, sliced
1 T. garlic powder

2 T. rosemary

    Wash and dry zucchini. Keep them whole until ready to use. Bag in zippered vegetable bag. Bag garlic powder and rosemary together.

Mud Volcano Hasty-Pudding

1/2 bag semisweet chocolate chips   **4** sponge shortcakes
1 orange

Bag ingredients separately. Pack orange with other fruit.

In-the-field preparation

Open and drain chicken and oysters, placing discarded liquid in a used plastic bag for disposal. Finely chop chicken and oysters. Mix them in a small bowl with parsley and lemon peel. In a separate large bowl, mix together cooked rice in a large bowl with cheese, butter, nutmeg, and mace. Slowly add light cream until a dough forms. Rub some flour on the cutting board and rolling pin. Place a large spoonful of rice dough on the cutting board and roll out to a circle of about six inches that is approximately 1/4 inch thick. Spoon chicken mix onto half of the circle, fold in half over the chicken mixture and seal with a fork by mashing down the edges. Set on a plate. Repeat until all the dough and chicken mixture have been used up. Heat oil in a large skillet over medium heat. Beat egg in a small bowl. Brush each rice cake with egg and roll in cornmeal. Fry until golden brown, approximately 4–5 minutes, turning once. Place on paper towels to drain. Slice zucchini. Pour 1 c. water into a medium saucepan. Place steamer basket filled with zucchini in an overlapping layer pattern. Sprinkle with garlic/rosemary mixture. Cover and heat over medium heat until steam rises. Serve on plate with rice cakes. For dessert, divide sponge shortcakes into individual bowls. Grate the peel from half the orange. Cut orange in half and squeeze juice and pulp into a small saucepan. Add grated peel and chocolate chips. Heat on low, stirring constantly, until chips begin to melt. Pour into the wells in the shortcakes. Serve.

AS AN OPTION on all other types of trips, dehydrate meats and vegetables. Substitute powdered milk (or condensed milk on all but the backpacking trips). Brush rice cakes with powdered egg dissolved in water instead of using a fresh egg.

Approaching one of the bubbling "cauldrons" near Mud Volcano, Langford, who must have been famished at the time, decided the cooking mass "of the consistency of thick paint" with "some being yellow, others pink, and others dark brown" "boiling at a fearful rate" did so "much after the fashion of a hasty-pudding in the last stages of completion." Thankfully, our hasty-pudding tastes of chocolate, not mud.

DAY SEVEN MENU

Breakfast

Judge Walls' Beefy Breakfast
Toast with Raspberries
Coffee and Juice

Lunch

Swinging Bridge
Breadsticks
Grapes
Tea

Dinner

Wedding of the Waters
Hot City Shorts
Boysen Banger
Ale, Tea and/or Milk

189

DAY SEVEN

My whispered word "elk" gets everyone up silently. The chilly dawn air smells crisp and piney. Connor, Linda, and Mandy quietly emerge from the tents. Half a dozen elk cross the road near us. Linda flips her video camera to night vision and films their unhurried progress. One by one, their distinctive white rumps disappear into the forest behind us. What a fantastic way to begin the last day of our car camping adventure!

In Cody's early days, Judge W. L. Walls sat on the bench, reputed to possess "a sarcastic humor which has made many culprits squirm." A man accused of stealing and butchering beef appeared before the judge. The accused explained that he couldn't have possibly brought the stolen beef into town, "owing to the fact that his two pack-horses were heavily loaded with other things." Of course, the judge demanded an accounting of the items. The accused snapped back with one horse loaded down with his fur overcoat, mining equipment, and tools; however, he became increasingly flustered when trying to name what the second horse carried. All the accused could come up with was "a gallon of whisky," to which the judge dryly replied, "I knew a gallon of whiskey was a load for a man, but I didn't know it was a load for a horse."

Day Seven Breakfast Recipe

Judge Walls' Beefy Breakfast

4 thin slices of veal	**1** t. black pepper
6 eggs	**1** small lemon
3 T. flour	**1** t. capers
1/2 c. oil	**2** T. butter

Freeze veal. Bag flour and pepper together in a gallon-size zipper bag. Pack remaining ingredients separately. Can pack lemon with other fruit.

Toast with Raspberries

whole wheat bread   **1** pt. box fresh raspberries

Wash and dry raspberries. Bag in zippered vegetable bag. Bag bread separately.

In-the-field preparation

In a large skillet heat oil over medium heat. Beat 2 eggs in a bowl with a whisk. Dip veal slices one at a time in eggs, then drop in the bag containing flour, coating veal well.

Cook veal in the skillet, turning once to brown both sides. Preheat tailgate oven to 200°F. Remove veal when done and keeping them warm in the oven. Pour skillet drippings into a small saucepan. Cut lemon in half and squeeze the juice from 1/2 into the pan. Add capers and 1 c. water. Wipe out skillet and reheat with 2 T. butter over medium heat. Whisk 4 eggs together in a bowl and pour into the skillet. Cook. Divide among individual plates and serve with veal. Raise oven temperature to 400°F and toast bread. Serve with raspberries.

THIS MEAL *can be served for a first night dinner on horse, goat, and float trips. Choose another option when backpacking.*

Buffalo Bill, the perpetual promoter, insisted the town be named Cody. He wanted it to become the perfect gem city of the Rockies, a place that offered sophistication to world travelers and, at the same time, a bustling hub that would accommodate ranchers, settlers, and sportsmen. He got his wish, and his mark can be seen on just about everything around. We drive pass the Buffalo Bill Reservoir created out of the canyon on the Shoshone River between the Cedar and Rattlesnake mountains, dammed up by the Buffalo Bill Dam. Completed in 1910, the 325-foot dam was, at the time, the tallest in the world.

We don't stop. Instead we push ahead until we reach the turnout for Colter's Hell beyond the other side of the reservoir. Many historians inaccurately associate the "legend of Colter's Hell" with all his "tall tales" about "roaring mountains" and "boiling springs" belonging to Yellowstone's mythology. Nonetheless, in 1807, he actually did come across this spot near the North and South Forks of the Shoshone River that now bears the name Colter's Hell. In 1837, Washington Irving described the volcanic district that in Colter's day spewed odious gases, rumbled, and its cauldrons boiled up water and mud as a "volcanic tract," "its gloomy terrors, its hidden fires, smoking pits, noxious steams and the all-prevailing 'smell of brimstone'" that haunted "the Stinking Waters" as the Shoshone River had been labeled on William Clark's map. Today, the almost extinct geysers present a colorful reminder of some controversial history.

Linda drags her brother back to the car, and we blow through town like the ever-present breeze. She was willing to forego spending the day wandering through the fabulous museums, named after Buffalo Bill in order to spend the afternoon swimming in the hot springs at Thermopolis. The town sits in the bottom of the Big Horn Basin enclosed by the Big Horn Mountains on the east, the Owl Creek Range on the south, the Pryors and Beartooths on the north, and the Absarokas on the west. Thermopolis received its name due to the hot springs. It means "hot city" in Greek.

Considering the amount and variety of dinosaurs' bones found around the basin, Bahguewana, pronounced băh GWĀY wă nă, which means "smoking waters" in the Shoshone language, has drawn soakers to its renowned healing waters for a very long time. Legend tells of a young indigenous couple who walked up to the top of the rock cliffs at the mouth of Wind River Canyon. A sudden breeze came up and pulled the feather from the woman's hair. It wafted gently down into the basin below. The couple followed it, and where it landed, a hot spring formed. After bathing in its mineral waters, they returned to their people and told them of the hot springs. Indigenous people have been coming to Bahguewana ever since. The hot springs were among the lands set aside for the Wind River Indian Reservation; however, ranchers and homesteaders coveted the land. In 1896, Chief Washakie, Arapaho chief Sharp Nose, among other, signed a treaty that gave the U.S. government ten square miles surrounding Bahguewana. The treaty, however, contained two stipulations. A portion of the hot springs must always remain free for anyone to use and a camping spot would be reserved for tribal members to stay for free while using the hot springs. The result was the formation of Hot Springs State Park.

We park near the state-run bathhouse, then walk up the trail to the Bahguewana, the Big Spring. From a gangplank-style overlook, we can peer down into the big bluish green cauldron as it churns out over three million gallons of water a day, maintaining a temperature between 127 and 135 degrees Fahrenheit. Rain and snowmelt percolate through the rock layers of the Owl Creek Mountains and flow into underground formations to the location of the hot springs. Subterranean volcanic gasses and chemicals from the rocks mix with the water, heating it. Then it boils to the surface. From there Connor, Linda, and I cross the Big Horn River on the suspension foot bridge. Locals refer to it as the "swinging bridge" for good reason. Mandy wants no part of it and waits for us near the footpath that winds between the Rainbow Terrace and the riverfront. Out over the river as the bridge gently sways beneath our feet, we take in an unmatched view of magnificently hued travertine terraces that formed over centuries from mineral deposits building up along the path the water from Bahguewana takes to the Big Horn River, made even more spectacular by being set against a backdrop of hills of deep red shales from the Triassic age Chugwater formation dating back to as far as 245 million years ago. Rejoining Mandy on the paved pathway along the terrace, we get an up-close look at several species of algae and plankton, well suited to surviving in the rivulets of hot water. They and the minerals in the water give the terraces a rainbow of colors.

Back in the parking lot, the kids race off to find a picnic table. Mandy and I gather up the canned goods for our lunch. *The Ladies' Home Journal* in 1907 insisted that canned foods had become "a universal solvent that will turn the grossness of the kitchen drudgery into the pure gold of pleasure. There is a witchery in cooking with canned goods that is positively fascinating." Once the cook began experiments with the one hundred varieties of canned foods available on the market, the sky was the limit. Choices included the every popular canned ox tongue, lamb's tongue, and extract of beef. Our canned goods are tame in comparison.

Day Seven Lunch Recipe

Swinging Bridge

3 carrots, grated

1 15 oz. can sweet peas

1 10.75 oz. can tomato soup

1 18.5 oz. can split pea soup

1 t. black pepper

1/2 c. sherry

1 pkg. breadsticks

Wash grapes and take off stems. When dry bag in a zippered vegetable bag. Bag breadsticks. Pack remaining ingredients separately.

In-the-field preparation

Drain peas and discard liquid. Pour them and both soups into a medium saucepan. Grate carrots and add to soups. Add pepper. Heat over low heat, stirring occasionally, until hot. Remove from heat. Add sherry. Serve with breadsticks.

AS AN OPTION, dehydrate carrots and skip the sherry and, if you don't mind the extra weight, this meal works well on horse, goat, float, and backpacking trips.

Once we finish lunch, we hit the pools. Linda and Connor delight in the water slide that splashdowns in the outdoor pool cooled down to a comfortable 104 degrees. Laughing at their antics, Mandy and I relax in the soothing mineral waters.

Late in the afternoon, we take a circuitous route out of the park so we can catch a glimpse at the "Monarch of the Plains." The park's herd of bison ranges around twenty-five adults. We're lucky enough to spot some little light cinnamon-colored youngsters dashing around their mothers.

Next, we advance to our final wow of the journey, Wind River Canyon, located a few miles from town back on the Wind River Indian Reservation. We enter the canyon at the "Wedding of the Waters." When early surveyors mapped the area, they mistook the bend in the Wind River for it merging with another, they had named the Big Horn River, hence the quaint moniker. In 1899, Tom Hall likened the fierce flow of the river to "a squadron at the charge." Erosion from the water and human disturbance in constructing the highway along one side of the river and the railroad bed on the opposite side have exposed a billion years of history set in stone. Fortunately, when the state widened the highway in the 1960s, they had the forethought to add strategically placed turnouts and later signage for a casual geological tour through the canyon.

After passing by more Chugwater Formation, we enter the canyon. The striking crossbedded white, buff, tan, and gray of the Tensleep Sandstone and the interbedded gray and white limestone, chert, and shale in the Phosphoria Formation of Permian Age form prominent cliffs at the north end of the canyon. They immediately draw our gaze. White and pink quartz and feldspar slice through dark metamorphic rock farther into the canyon. From a turnout just north of the one of the canyon's most spectacular features, we marvel at the three short tunnels blasted out of rose-colored pre-Cambrian era rock that dates from up to 4.6 billion years ago.

Just on the other side lies Boysen State Park. We camp beside its deep blue water of Boysen Reservoir at the south end of the canyon. After we set up camp, I get to work on dinner. As I slice mushrooms for the salad, Linda asks me about the difference between mushrooms and toad stools. The latter, of course, can be pretty deadly. Then again, so can certain mushrooms. Picking them in the wild requires extensive knowledge. So I'm thankful for the wealth available at grocery stores. I'm using button mushrooms to go with the spinach. In 1797, *The Time Piece and Literary Companion* ran an article explaining how to test mushrooms. It suggested cooking an onion with the mushrooms and if the onion turned black or bluish, poisonous mushrooms lurked amid the meal. If the onion "remains white, they are good." Considering that onions never remain white, turning transparent or brown depending on how you cook them, I'd take that old advice about mushrooms with a bucket of salt!

Day Seven Dinner Recipes

Wedding of the Waters

1/2 lb. sharp cheddar cheese

8 slices bread

1/2 t. dry mustard

1 t. paprika

1 c. ale

Bag all ingredients separately. Pack cheese in the ice chest when ready to leave on trip.

Hot City Shorts

1 bunch spinach
1 cucumber, sliced
1 8 oz. box mushrooms, sliced
1/2 small Bermuda onion, sliced

1 small jar green olives stuffed with pimentos
1 bottle Italian dressing

Wash and dry spinach and cucumber. Brush any dirt off mushroom, but do not wash. Pack all ingredients separately.

Boysen Banger

1 pt. blackberries
1 pt. strawberries

1/2 c. dark brown sugar
1/2 c. brandy

Wash and dry blackberries and strawberries. Bag together in a zippered vegetable bag. Pack remaining ingredients separately.

In-the-field preparation

Slice cucumber, onion, and mushrooms. Drain olives and discard liquid. In a large bowl, mix spinach leaves with cucumbers, onion, mushrooms, and olives. Drizzle Italian dressing over salad and toss. Set aside. Grate cheese into bowl. Fill lower saucepan of the double boiler about half full of water. Heat over medium heat. Preheat tailgate oven to 350°F. Cut each slice of bread diagonally into a wedge shape and toast until golden brown and crisp. Then turn off oven but leave toast inside to keep it warm. When water in lower pan is hot, slowly shake cheese into upper pan of double boiler, stirring with a whisk continuously, but slowly. When just about creamy, add mustard. Stir in well. Slowly add ale and continue to whisk until all ingredients are mixed together. Remove from heat. Arrange two pieces of bread on each plate and immediately spoon cheese mixture on top, sprinkle with paprika and serve with salad on the side. For dessert, slice strawberries. Divide them and blackberries into individual bowls. Heat the brandy and brown sugar in a saucepan over low heat until the sugar dissolves. Drizzle over fruit. Serve.

THIS MEAL needs no adaptation for a first night dinner on float, horse, goat, or backpacking trips, as long as you don't mind carrying the extra weight.

CHAPTER FIVE

RIVER-RUNNING THE "SERENE GREEN" FOR A WEEK

Of all outdoor journeys, float trips offer a unique advantage. The water carries all the weight. So if your taste buds veer toward champagne and caviar and you can squeeze them in the ice chest, go for it! You only have to worry about lugging that chest into and out of the boat. Float trips (and car camping) accord the widest range of eating possibilities as ice chests keep perishable foods fresh and drinks cold for several days. There's nothing like kicking off your sneakers, letting your feet dangle in the cool water, leaning back against a soft pile of sleeping bags, munching on crisp cucumber and watercress sandwiches, and listening to ice cubes clink in your tea while the world quietly drifts by. River trips run for the course of an afternoon up to a week or more. Our river running on the "Serene Green" takes a leisurely seven days.

FLOAT LUNCHES

With the exertion level more or less comparable to goat packing, plan on about 1/3 pound of lunchables per person per day. Choose from the list below or from any of the other trail lunches listed in this cookbook. Include a supply of fresh fruit, fruit juices, and sodas as well. Serve the following fillers on breads, assorted crackers, muffins, tortillas, bagels, or rolls.

SANDWICH AND CRACKER FILLERS

Apricots (canned) mashed with chopped walnuts

Baked beans mashed with catsup

Carrots (raw) grated with mashed canned peas

Cream cheese with sliced cucumbers and watercress

Hard-boiled eggs with stewed tomatoes

Peanut butter and chopped sweet pickles

Peanut butter with chopped dates

Pineapple (canned, crushed) with chopped pecans

Raisins chopped with orange sections

Salmon (canned) with tomato slices and Dijon mustard

Lady of the Lake Lunch (see recipe below)

Smoked sausages mashed with 1 7 oz. can Salsa Verde

Turkey Day Spread (recipe below)

Trin-Alcove Sandwich Filler (recipe below)

SEVEN DAYS OF FLOAT TRIP MEALS

Hints for taking fresh foods into the field:

Store onions and potatoes in net bags (like onions come in at the store). Do not seal them in plastic bags as it will promote sprouting or, worse yet, rot. Store apples and oranges separately as they each give off gases that aid in spoiling the other variety of fruit. Cover ice chests with tarps, duffel bags, or sleeping bags to keep them out of the direct sunlight. Since frequent opening of an ice chest causes the ice to melt quicker, put all perishable food and drink items for the first day in one ice chest. Store the second day's perishable food and drinks in a second chest, etc., and don't open until necessary. Tape shut all but the first day's ice chest with duct tape and number each chest in order of use. This keeps the chests from accidently coming open if turned over, plus it stops people from digging into the wrong food chest by mistake. To keep bread products from becoming soggy, store them in plastic containers with airtight lids on top of the ice. Also, use blocks of ice rather than cubes since block ice takes longer to melt. To avoid the possibility of losing all your food should a boat flip over, divide ice chests up between all the boats. The supply lists and recipes for this particular trip have been adjusted to accommodate for seven people under a semistrenuous work load.

SUPPLY LIST (7 DAYS)

Baking Staples

1 10 oz. box baking powder

1 16 oz. box baking soda

1 lb. blue cornmeal

5 lb. sack of flour

1 lb. can powdered buttermilk

1 25.6 oz. box powdered milk

1 8 oz. bag semisweet chocolate chips

5 lb. sack sugar

Canned Goods

2 2 oz. cans anchovies

1 10 oz. can baby clams in water

2 5 oz. can bamboo shoots

1 2.25 oz. chopped black olives

1 4 oz. can chopped green chilies

2 27 oz. can whole green chilies

1 16 oz. can jellied cranberry sauce

1 16 oz. can peach halves in juice

1 16 oz. can sliced peaches in juice

1 20 oz. can pineapple chunks in juice

1 20 oz. can pineapple rings in juice

1 16 oz. can tomato sauce

2 28 oz. cans diced tomato

3 5 oz. can water chestnuts

1 15 oz. can sweet peas

Breads/Crackers/Cereals

1 pkg. assorted individual boxes of cereal

1 box crisp rice cereal

10 bagels

2 pkg. English muffins

1 loaf sourdough bread

1 lb. box graham crackers

1 box crackers

1 bag corn chips

bread/rolls (prepoll trip participants for preferred bread and roll types)

Dried Fruit/Vegetables/Nuts

1 2 oz. pkg. almond slivers

1 lb. chopped walnuts

1 container candied fruits

1 8 oz. box chopped dates

1 14 oz. bag coconut flakes

1 lb. box raisins

Fresh Fruit

12 apples

8 bananas

4 lbs. grapes

1 honeydew melon

12 oranges

4 tomatoes

Fresh Vegetables

2 bell peppers
1 lb. carrots
1 bunch celery
1 cucumber
1 bunch watercress
1 clove garlic
1 eggplant
2 green chilies

1 bunch green onions
1 lb. mushrooms
1 lb. okra
6 onions
1 bunch green onions
12 potatoes
2 yellow squash

Frozen Food

1 16 oz. pkg. San Francisco-style vegetables

Meat/Milk/Margarine/Cheese/Eggs

1 lb. bacon
2 lb. beef
2 lb. ham (1 lb. sliced paper thin)
1 lb thin sliced turkey lunch meat
2 lbs. turkey sausage
10 whole chicken breasts
2 8 oz. pkg. cream cheese

2 lb. Monterey Jack cheese
1/2 lb. Mizithra cheese
2 dozen eggs
2 12 oz. cans evaporated milk
2 lbs. margarine
1 qt. olive oil

Rice/Noodles

2 lb. brown rice
2 12 oz. pkg. egg noodles

2 7 oz. pkg. rice sticks
1 22 oz. pkg. spaghetti

Sauce & Other Mixes/Drinks/Specialty Items

1 bottle soy sauce
1 bottle Worcestershire sauce
1 8 oz. can Amaretto flavored coffee drink
1 1.58 oz. anchovy paste
1 jar beef bouillon cubes
2 12 oz can beer
1 3 1/2 oz. jar caviar

1 jar Chinese Hot Mustard
1 jar Dijon mustard
1 qt. cranberry juice
2 6 oz. custard-style strawberry yogurt
1 lb. jar honey
1 6 oz. jar maraschino cherries
1 lb. bag miniature marshmallows
1 12 oz. bag Semisweet chocolate chips

1 bottle molasses
1 10 oz. jar peach jam
1 bottle ranch dressing

60 assorted tea bags, coffee, soda pop
(optional)
fruit juice (optional)

Spices

1 container allspice
1 container cayenne pepper
1 container cinnamon
1 container cumin
1 container dry mustard
1 container coarse black pepper
1 container garlic powder
1 container ginger

1 container ground cloves
1 container mace
1 container onion powder
1 container parsley flakes
1 container pepper
1 container salt
1 container thyme

Miscellaneous

Easy-light charcoal briquettes

DAY ONE MENU

Breakfast

Ham Haystack

Myzithra Cheese

Coffee

Lunch

Carrots (raw) Grated with Mashed Canned Peas

Cream Cheese with Sliced Cucumbers and Watercress

Fresh Fruit

Juice or Soda

Dinner

River Runner's Chicken

San Rafael Cake

Tea

DAY ONE

July 13. This afternoon our way is through a valley with cottonwood groves on either side. The river is deep, broad, and quiet.

—John Wesley Powell

John Wesley Powell, a geologist, led the first expedition down the Green and Colorado rivers in 1869. On July 13, the four boats in the expedition pulled ashore for an afternoon break about five miles south of where we put in at the Green River State Park in Utah. Powell kept a daily journal on long, narrow strips of brown paper which he bound in shoe sole leather. When he published his log in 1895, he maintained he hadn't undertaken the exploration for adventure, but "purely for scientific purposes." But we, on the other hand, set out on a rainy May day to retrace 120 miles of his trip from Green River, Utah, to just past the confluence of the Green and Colorado rivers solely for adventure.

The 1869 crew consisted of ten men, not a greenhorn among them. Experience in our group of eight ranges from long-time white water runners to weekend floaters to a never-been-in-a-boat beginner. Alan and Bobby, cousins, wanted to test the waters as a team before they tackle the white water through the Grand Canyon. Ty and Erin figure a canoe trip down what river runners called the "Serene Green" will make for a memorable honeymoon. Lance, a businessman, loves the idea of a week in the inaccessible Canyonlands with no cell phone or Internet. Then there is Ron, our guide, who grew up on the river, and me, the hired cook.

The gang shuttles vehicles and boat trailers over to Moab, fifty-two miles from Green River and arranges for a jet boat to meet us at the confluence. Seven days hence, it will haul us and the canoes sixty miles up the Colorado to our waiting cars. I stay behind to finish packing the food, adding a last bit of ice, taping down the chests, and marking the ration days on the lids.

Early in the 1859 trip Powell took the rations for granted, not even listing the amount of food taken on board. Instead he wrote, "We take with us rations deemed sufficient to last ten months." Only later, when they ran into hardships did meals become the subject of journal entries. By the time our crew return, I have breakfast ready.

Day One Breakfast Recipe

Ham Haystack

1/2 lb. paper-thin sliced ham

4 T. course black pepper

1 T. allspice

sourdough bread

Mix pepper and allspice. Sprinkle some over each slice of ham, gently patting into the meat. Stack slices. Freeze. Also freeze 1 loaf of sourdough bread. Pack cheese.

In-the-field preparation

While water boils for coffee, layer some ham on bread slices. Serve with cheese.

THIS MEAL requires no adaptation for use on horse, goat, or car camping trips as a first-day breakfast. It's suitable for a first-day breakfast on a backpack trip if you don't mind some extra weight.

Although we pack all gear in plastic garbage bags, we still bundle everything in dry bags, obtained from the army surplus store, before stowing them under tarps in the canoes. Cameras and film go in watertight ammo boxes. Then we tie everything to the boats just in case one of the four canoes flip over. Unlikely in such calm waters, but it can happen. Ropes offered peace of mind, as does dividing the food among the four boats just as Powell did.

Day One Lunch

1/2 lb. carrots (raw) grated

1 15 oz. can sweet peas

1 8 oz. pkg. cream cheese

1 cucumber

1 bunch watercress

1 box crackers

1 bag corn chips

fresh fruit (grapes, bananas, apples, or oranges)

juice or soda

Mix grated carrots and sweet peas. Mash and bag together. Chop cucumber and watercress. Mix with cream cheese and bag. Bag fruit. Pack crackers and/or chips.

In-the-field preparation

Spread carrot and pea filling on crackers or dip with chips. Spread cream cheese cucumber mix on crackers or dip with chips.

THIS MEAL requires no adaptation for use on horse or goat trips and car camping as a first-day lunch. It's suitable for a first-day lunch on a backpack trip if you don't mind some extra weight.

After eating our hurried lunch, we finally get underway. Slickers protect our bodies from a persistent rain. We continually swab the deck with thick sponges, but our sneakers soak up the cold water like thirsty desert travelers.

The dreary sky washes out the landscape, all but eradicating the distant cliffs on the horizon. Raindrops dimple the river. Wind kicks miniature waves against the boat hulls. Since none of us have canoed together before, each team concentrates on gaining a rhythm to paddling in sync. The boats fishtail in a few near misses until we get it figured out. Thunder ricochets off the sandstone butte, sounding ominous. Then the lightning starts. It discharges over Dellenbaugh Butte, named after Frederick Dellenbaugh, one of the young men who accompanied Powell on his second expedition in 1871. By general consensus, we decide to call it a day. We quickly pull in near where the San Rafael River streams into the Green. Alan and Bobby help Ron off-load gear while Ty, Erin, and Lance put up tents on wet sand.

I set up the two-burner stove under my folding table instead of on it and began heating water for hot drinks. At least we will have a hot meal, unlike Powell's crew who had to "weather out" a night of storms with no dinner. The next morning, Powell wrote that they had to "search for some time to find a few sticks of driftwood, just sufficient to boil a cup of coffee." All the driftwood littering the beach where we camp is soaked. When it comes time to bake our cake, I dump a layer of charcoal bricks over the top of the dutch oven and hold a lighter to them until they catch fire. Powell's men who missed their dinner would be so envious!

Day One Dinner Recipes

River Runner's Chicken

10 whole chicken breasts, deboned and sliced

1 10 oz. jar peach jam

1/3 c. cranberry juice

1 T. soy sauce

1 t. ginger

1 T. Worcestershire sauce

1 t. pepper

1 t. dry mustard

1 t. garlic powder

1 16 oz. pkg. frozen San Francisco-style vegetables

1 16 oz. can sliced peaches in juice

1 16 oz. can tomato sauce

1 22 oz. pkg. spaghetti

1 T. margarine

Marinate chicken in next 8 ingredients for 24 hours. Freeze (don't drain marinade before freezing). Cook spaghetti in 2 qts. boiling water, uncovered, for 12 minutes. Remove from heat. Drain. Mix cooked spaghetti with frozen vegetables and peaches in their juice, bag and freeze. Store margarine separately.

San Rafael Cake

1 1/3 c. flour

1/3 c. sugar

1 t. salt

1 t. baking powder

1 t. baking soda

1 T. ginger

1/2 c. chopped walnuts

1/4 c. powdered milk

1/4 c. plus 2 T. margarine

Bag together all ingredients except margarine.

In-the-field preparation

Cut 1/4 c. margarine into dry cake ingredients. Add 1/3 c. cold water. Reseal bag and squeeze to mix. Makes a stiff dough. Melt 2 T. margarine in Dutch oven or skillet. Spread dough in it. Cover. Bake over low heat with a lid fire for 25–30 minutes. Melt margarine in the skillet. Add chicken, cover and cook until done. Stir in vegetable/fruit mixture, cooking over medium heat until vegetables are thoroughly heated. Serve.

AS AN OPTION on backpacking trips, grind, brown, and dehydrate the meat after marinating it. Also dehydrate the vegetables. On horse or goat trips, this meal can be carried as is and served the first day out, or follow the backpacking option. No adaptation is needed for car camping.

DAY TWO MENU

Breakfast

Rushing River Bagels

Tea

Lunch

Turkey Day Spread

Trin-Alcove Sandwich Filler

Fruit

Juice or soda

Dinner

Green Chile Relleno

Blue Corn Bread

Grapes

DAY TWO

July 15. Three side canyons enter at the same point. These canyons are very tortuous, almost closed in from view, and, seen from the opposite side of the river, they appear like three alcoves. We name this Trin-Alcove Bend. . . . The right cove is a narrow, winding gorge, with overhanging walls, almost shutting out the light. The left is an amphitheater, turning spirally up, with overhanging shelves. A series of basins filled with water are seen at different altitudes as we pass by; huge rocks are piled below on the right, and overhead there is an arched ceiling."

—**John Wesley Powell**

In 1869, Powell's crew lived on coffee, sugar, jerky, apples, biscuits, dried beans, and bacon that was too greasy to store in the rubber bags they used to supposedly keep the supplies dry. Despite precautions, the dried beans turned soggy from repeated dunkings in the muddy water, finally sprouting. Likewise, the apples began to ferment, and flour for biscuits became hopelessly moldy. No wonder three of Powell's men mutinied!

Day Two Breakfast Recipe

Rushing River Bagels

10 plain bagels
1 8 oz. pkg. cream cheese

1 3 1/2 oz. jar caviar
2 eggs

Pack each item separately.

In-the-field preparation

Bring eggs to a boil in a covered, large pot of cold water, 3–5 minutes. Remove from heat and let stand for 20 minutes. Reserve water for tea if eggs remain unbroken. Lightly toast bagel halves face down in the skillet over medium heat. Spread cream cheese on each bagel half. Top with 1/8 t. of the caviar. Peel and slice eggs, placing one slice of egg on top of each bagel half. Serve with tea.

THIS MEAL is only suitable as a first breakfast on either horse or goat trips. Substitute a less perishable breakfast for backpacking. No adaptation is needed for car camping.

Pools high in the rocks of the Trin-Alcove have continued to provide river runners with a great source for fresh water since Powell first wrote about them. We fill every empty container, knowing we can't count on drinking from the Green. The river carries an estimated nineteen tons of silt per year, making the water the color and consistency of Cajun gumbo. All those particles defeat filters, clogging them quickly. Even in 1869, Powell searched for pools of rain water standing in holes in the rocks to fill the team's need for drinking water.

Scrub brush shores and a series of variegated-colored buttes start to swell into canyon walls by afternoon, tall, formidable slabs of burnt orange sandstone. Neither Powell nor Dellenbaugh mentioned feeling dwarfed by the steep canyons, but I do. The others must feel it too because chatter ceases. Only the song of a wren and the cry of a hawk intrude into the brooding quiet.

Due to the Green's placid flow, we spend much of the day dipping and swinging paddles. But as lunchtime rolls around, we follow in a tradition begun by Powell's expedition. Steering the canoes toward each other until all crafts cluster side by side, we "tie" (Powell used real ropes for this) the boats together by draping our feet and arms into neighboring canoes to stop us from drifting apart. In this manner, we enjoy our lunch. (I had made sure the ingredients were easily accessible before we shoved off this morning.)

Day Two Lunch Recipes

Turkey Day Spread

1 6 oz. pkg. thin sliced turkey lunch
   meat, shredded
1 16 oz. can jellied cranberry sauce

2 stalks celery, chopped fine
1 t. onion powder

> *Blend well. Store in a zipper bag.*

Trin-Alcove Sandwich Filler

2 apples, chopped fine
2 stalks celery, chopped fine
1/3 c. nuts, chopped

1 2.25 oz. can chopped black olives,
   drained
3 T. ranch dressing
Rolls

> *Mix all ingredients. Add more dressing if needed to hold spread together. Serve on rolls.*
>
> **THIS LUNCH** *is only suitable for a first-day lunch on horse and goat trips, or for backpacking if you don't mind the extra weight. No adaptation is needed for car camping.*

In the late afternoon, twentieth-century petroglyphs catch our attention and imagination—especially the ghostly image of the *The Face of the River*. Its age and the identity of the artist who chiseled the face and flowing body high on a sandstone wall remains a mystery. The carving's bug-eyes watch the river far below, observing all who drift by on the slow current. He tallies their names in his River Register, the names and years of Green River expeditions etched in stone. Some date back to the early 1900s.

We make camp on the south side of Bowknot Bend, a nine mile loop in the river that takes you back to within six hundred yards of its beginning. While Powell's crew ate supper spread out on a beach in this vicinity, he noted, "We name this Labyrinth Canyon." I dig a shallow pit in the terrace of sand at the base of the cliff, throw in some charcoal bricks, and light a fire. After I mix up the cornbread, I pour it into a greased cast iron dutch oven. Scraping some coals to the side with the shovel, I create a flat bed to set the pot on. The piled up coals then get shoveled evenly (for uniform baking) onto the lid of the Dutch oven. Since heat rises and the bottom will cook quicker, I maintain a hotter fire on the lid, adding more coals as they burn to ash. When the bread browns around the edge and the center bounces back when lightly touched, it's ready. Powell's cook called his dutch oven an "iron bake-oven" and used it primarily for biscuits.

Day Two Dinner Recipes

Green Chile Relleno

2 27 oz. can whole green chilies

2 1 lb. Monterey Jack cheese, sliced

3 c. flour

4 eggs

2 12 oz. beer

3 c. plus 1 T. olive oil

2 28 oz. can diced tomatoes

1 T. cinnamon

1 1/2 c. rice

Pack each item separately. Beer doesn't need to be cold. Put oil in plastic bottle.

Blue Corn Bread

1 c. blue cornmeal

2/3 c. flour

1/4 c. powdered milk

1 T. sugar

1 t. baking powder

1 t. salt

1/2 t baking soda

1 4 oz. can chopped green chilies

1 T. margarine

Mix together and bag all ingredients except chilies and margarine.

Grapes

Pick firm, fresh grapes. Wash and remove from the stem. Pat dry and store in a vegetable zipper bag.

In-the-field preparation

In a medium covered saucepan, bring rice and 1 1/2 c. water to boil over high head. Add 1/4 c. more cold water and reduce heat to low. Simmer, covered, 20–25 minutes. Meanwhile, add undrained 4 oz. can chopped peppers and 1 c. water to dry corn bread ingredients. Melt margarine in skillet. Spread dough in skillet. Bake with a lid fire for 30 minutes. Heat 2 c. oil in skillet, (reserve 1 c. oil to add as needed). Open whole chilies and drain. Stuff with cheese. Mix flour, eggs, beer, and 1 T. oil together. Dip chilies one at a time in the batter, completely coating them. Fry in oil until brown, flipping once. Repeat until all chilies are cooked. Open diced tomatoes and pour into smaller pot. Add cinnamon and bring to a boil. Serve over the stuffed peppers. Serve grapes for dessert.

THIS MEAL *requires no adaptation for car camping, horse, or goat trips. To make the Chile Relleno suitable for backpacking, make them in the form of pancakes. Dehydrate chopped chilies, omit eggs, replace beer with 1 1/3 c. powdered milk and water, replace oil with 2 T. melted margarine to be used in the batter and 2 T. to fry the cakes in. Replace canned tomatoes with 4 fresh ones that have been chopped and dried. Replace grapes with raisins.*

211

DAY THREE MENU

Breakfast
Labyrinth Eggs
Coffee

Lunch
Peanut Butter and Chopped Sweet Pickle Sandwiches
Pineapple (Canned, Crushed) with
Chopped Pecans Sandwiches
Juice or Soda

Dinner
Outlaw Stew
Bowknot

DAY THREE

July 15. There is an exquisite charm in our ride today down this beautiful canyon. It gradually grows deeper with every mile of travel; the walls are symmetrically curved and grandly arched, of a beautiful color, and reflected in the quiet waters in many places so as almost to deceive the eye and suggest to the beholder the thought that he is looking into profound depths. We are all in fine spirits and feel very gay, and the badinage of men is echoed from wall to wall. Now and then we whistle or shout or discharge a pistol, to listen to the reverberations among the cliffs.

—**John Wesley Powell**

While I prepare breakfast, Ron leads the party up on top of the Bowknot for a bird's-eye view of the huge bend in the river. One of the times Powell's crew awaited his return from an exploratory jaunt, they succeeded in catching a good, but unmentioned number of fish. "This is a delightful addition to our *menu*," the leader logged less than a month into the trip. I wonder if his stressing the word "menu" came as a result of the men tiring of the rations.

Day Three Breakfast Recipe

Labyrinth Eggs

12 eggs
1 1.58 oz. tube anchovy paste
1 16 oz. can tomato sauce
Pack each item separately.

2 T. pepper
2 T. parsley flakes
8 English muffins

In-the-field preparation

Warm English muffin halves while boiling water for coffee by placing them on the lid of the water pot (or in the skillet with a two-burner stove). Heat skillet. Break eggs into it. Add 2 c. water. Cover and steam over medium heat until eggs are cooked. Spread anchovy paste over the English muffins. Top each half with an egg. Pour tomato sauce over egg. Sprinkle with pepper and parsley. Serve.

THIS MEAL needs no adaptation for horse, car camping, or goat trips, or for backpacking if you take the eggs in a special container and don't mind the extra weight.

We get underway, but within half an hour, a cold rain lashes us, falling in heavy sheets. The surface of the river rings with droplets. No immediate spot presents itself for us to land and dig slickers out of the dry bags. Then Lance glimpses a sliver-sized sandbar at the base of a cliff. We angle over to it and beach the boats. Of course, by the time we don our slickers and get back on the water, the rain quits.

As we paddle through Canyonlands, the enormity of time soaks into my bones. With patient perseverance and endurance, the river has cut its way through one thousand feet of rock. The walls look like temples on crumbling foundations. Blind arches abound, created by rain seeping into tiny crevices in the cliffs, gnawing away the stone bit by bit until entire slabs break free and crash into talus fields at the wall's footing or get swallowed up by the river below.

By lunchtime, the sun glitters off the water like thousands of fireflies. Cotton-woods hang over the bank, their delicate green leaves dancing in the current. We put in at Mineral Canyon Bottoms and enjoy a picnic at the head of a draw that mean-ders into the side canyon. During the 1950s, a commercial uranium mine basked in the post–World War II boom. Burros and wagons hauled out ten tons of ore over one of the few access roads into the lower canyon area, an iffy four-wheel drive, high-ground clearance kind of road these days. Now only some rusted relics remain as reminders of this era.

Tonight we camp on a large, elongated island at Fort Bottom. Once we unload the gear and set up camp, we all pile into a couple of the canoes and cross to the

"mainland" to explore the historic sites found there. It's an easy climb up a dusty, nondescript path to "Outlaw Cabin." Rumor places it as a way station for the infamous Butch Cassidy. This inconspicuous log cabin, posing as a homesteader's abode, sits on a bench across the river from the once well-used trail leading to Brown's Hole or Hole-in-the-Wall.

On the pinnacle above the cab-in stands a lookout tower believed to be built over a century before by an indigenous nation called the Fremont Indians by the Americans. The structure is constructed entire-ly out of native, flat stones laid with no mortar to hold them together. Two small circular rooms remain intact, with part of a third still visible. The sun starts to set, bathing the landscape in fiery reds and oranges. Crickets begin their nightly rhapsody as we glide back to the island and a dinner of Outlaw Stew. After a similar excursion, Powell wrote, "Now we return to camp. While eating supper we very naturally speak of better fare, as musty bread and spoiled bacon are not palatable."

Day Three Dinner Recipes

Outlaw Stew

1 lb. bacon

6 potatoes

2 onions

6 carrots

2 t. pepper

2 T. parsley flakes

Pack bacon and carrots in ice chest for day three. Store onions and potatoes in net bags. Pack pepper shaker and a bag of parsley.

Bowknot

5 c. crisp rice cereal

2 c. miniature marshmallows

3/4 c. candied fruits

2 T. margarine

Bag each item separately.

In-the-field preparation

Lay strips of bacon in the bottom of the skillet, covering it. Slice vegetables. Put a layer of potato on top of the bacon. Sprinkle on some pepper and parsley. Add a layer of onion then a layer of carrots. Repeat until all ingredients are used. Pour 3 c. water over the top. Cover and bring to a boil. Simmer 30 minutes or until potatoes and bacon are cooked. DO NOT stir. Add water if necessary to keep from burning. Serve. While stew cooks (if you have a two-burner stove along), melt 1 T. margarine in a large pot. Add marshmallows, stirring until melted. Stir in cereals and fruit. Coat skillet with 1 T. margarine. Spread marshmallow mixture in skillet. Allow to set up for 10 minutes. Cut and serve.

AS AN OPTION on backpacking trips, cook, dry, and crumble bacon. Dehydrate potatoes, onions, and carrots. On horse and goat trips, this meal is suitable as is for the first day. If you plan to use it later in the trip, substitute canned or dried bacon. No adaptation is needed for car camping.

DAY FOUR MENU

Breakfast

Potatoes Canyonlands

Coffee

Lunch

Baked Beans Mashed with Catsup

Salmon (Canned) with Tomato Slices and Dijon Mustard

Fruit

Juice or Soda

Dinner

Stillwater Spaghetti

White Rim Oranges

DAY FOUR

July 17. We are now down among the buttes, and in a region the surface of which is naked, solid rock––a beautiful red sand stone, forming a smooth, undulating pavement. The Indians call this the "Toom'pin Tuweap", or Land of Standing Rock." Off to the south we see a butte in the form of a fallen cross. It is several miles away, but it presents no inconspicuous figure on the landscape and must be many hundreds of feet high, probably more than 2,000. We note its position on our map and name it "The Butte of the Cross."

—John Wesley Powell

The luxury of fresh fruit on a float trip was inconceivable in 1869. Even dehydrated fruits faired poorly. "The few pounds of dried apples have been spread in the sun and reshrunken to their normal dried bulk," wrote Powell after their apples got soaked in the river.

Day Four Breakfast Recipe

Potatoes Canyonlands

2 lb. turkey sausage

4 potatoes

6 green onions, chopped

2 apple

1 29 oz. can tomato sauce

1/2 t. cayenne pepper

2 T. margarine

Brown sausage. Dehydrate sausage and onions. Bag with cayenne pepper. Store potatoes, apple, tomato sauce, and margarine separately.

In-the-field preparation

Rehydrate sausage mixture. Melt margarine in a skillet. Grate potatoes. Sauté potatoes with sausage and onion. Chop apple. Add to the sausage. When done, add tomato sauce. Serve.

THIS MEAL needs no adaptation on car camping, horse, or goat trips. For backpacking, replace canned tomato sauce with 2 chopped and dried fresh tomatoes.

The Butte of the Cross dominates the vista for many miles before we reach it at lunchtime. We drift past it, the canoes nested together while we eat. Then the unthinkable happens. We hear the unmistakable rush of white water, and our hearts start pounding. Our river guidebook says nothing about rough water ahead, and Ron's forehead creases in a deep frown. We scramble to untangle the canoes and paddle through a corridor of buff-colored cliff walls straining to touch the sky. It's a false alarm. The cliffs have captured the sound of rifles and small haystacks (disturbances in the water caused by rocks beneath the surface) and bounce the noise up and down the canyon until we're sure we face uncharted white water within the confines of Stillwater Canyon. It makes us realize the thrill and the terror Powell and his men must have experienced.

We make an early day of it, putting in on the beach at Valentine Bottom. Above the sandy shore, bands of rusted sandstone and shale fade into the White Rim, the local name for the uppermost fringe of sandstone in Stillwater Canyon.

Once we set up camp, we eagerly dig into the crunchy canned vegetables in our Stillwater Spaghetti. For want of some vegetables, the 1869 expedition gathered some "potato tops" from an indigenous trader's garden, thinking the greens might make a nice change from their "salt-meat fare." "We stop and cook our greens for dinner; but soon one after another of the party is taken sick," Powell noted, finding out the hard way that only the tubers are edible.

Day Four Dinner Recipes

Stillwater Spaghetti

1 lb. beef, sliced thin
10 mushrooms, sliced
2 stalks celery, chopped
1 bell pepper, chopped
3 T. Chinese Hot Mustard

1 beef bouillon cube
2 5 oz. can bamboo shoots
2 5 oz. can sliced water chestnuts
2 7 oz. pkg. rice sticks

Marinate meat in the mustard that has been thinned with 3 T. of water. Dehydrate meat, mushrooms, bell pepper, and celery. Bag together with bouillon cube. Pack bamboo shoots, chestnuts, and rice sticks.

White Rim Oranges

4 oranges
1 2 oz. pkg. almond slivers

1 c. sugar
8 graham crackers

Store each item separately.

In-the-field preparation

Rehydrate meat mixture. Bring to a boil with 1 c. water in a covered pot. Add bamboo shoots and chestnuts. Simmer, stirring frequently until everything is tender. Meanwhile, bring another pot of water to boil. Add rice sticks. Cook for three minutes. Drain. Serve meat mixture over rice sticks. For dessert, peel oranges and chop three of them. Squeeze the juice from the fourth one into the smaller pot, reserving pulp to chop and add with the rest. Dissolve sugar in the juice. Bring to a boil, stirring constantly until sugar mixture thickens and boils. Add oranges and almonds. Return to a boil. Boil 2 minutes, stirring constantly. Divide graham crackers and crush into the small bowls. Pour oranges over them and serve.

__AS AN OPTION__ on backpack trips, dehydrate canned vegetables. If you don't wish to carry the extra weight of the oranges, choose another lightweight dessert. For car camping, horse, and goat trips, no adaptation is required.

DAY FIVE MENU

Breakfast

Lazy Water Cereal

Fruit

Coffee

Lunch

Hard Boiled Eggs with Stewed Tomatoes

Lady of the Lake Lunch

Juice or Soda

Dinner

Turk's Head Ham

Cherry Challenger

Tea

DAY FIVE

July 17. When thinking of these rocks one must not conceive of piles of boulders or heaps of fragments, but of a whole land of naked rock, with giant forms carved on it: cathedral-shaped buttes, towering hundreds or thousands of feet, cliffs that cannot be scaled, and canyon walls that shrink the river into insignificance, with vast, hollow domes and tall pinnacles and shafts set on the verge overhead; and all highly colored-buff, gray, red, brown, and chocolate— never lichened, never moss-covered, but bare, and often polished.

—John Wesley Powell

Powell found it necessary to cache food along the route, where possible. A cave near a creek that fed into the Green provided one such reserve. When the men arrived at it, they found a party of indigenous people had been camped close to the cache for several weeks and worried that their supplies would no longer be there. "Our fears are soon allayed, for find the cache undisturbed," Powell wrote upon returning to camp.

Day Five Breakfast Recipe

Lazy Water Cereal

assorted individual boxes of cereal   **3** 12 oz. cans evaporated milk

Bag in your usual serving sizes. Pack cans of milk.

In-the-field preparation

While water boils for coffee, open milk and mix with water until desired drinking consistency (no more than equal parts of milk and water). Pour cereal in bowls. Add milk. Serve with assorted fruits.

THIS MEAL needs no adaptation for horse, goat, or car camping trips. For backpacking, substitute powdered milk and dried fruit.

In 1869, the water flowed faster through Stillwater Canyon. "Late in the afternoon," Powell recorded, "the water becomes swift and our boats make great speed." On the other hand, we creep along, spending the morning and most of the afternoon linked together, content to drift. The day is desert hot, the sun relentless. We guzzle cans of fruit juice and get into paddle fights, batting dirty water on each other as a cooling down strategy. Bobby and Alan stage a mock sword fight with their paddle handles, almost tipping their canoe over as they duck and lunge at each other. Lunch offers a welcome break as it did for Powell's team. While tied together, drifting, they often read from Scott's *Lady of the Lake*. We read excerpts from Powell's trip instead.

Day Five Lunch Recipe

Lady of the Lake Lunch

2 2 oz. cans anchovies

3 T. Chinese Hot Mustard

1/4 t. cayenne pepper

1 T. parsley flakes

2 T. margarine

choice of breads or crackers

Bag cayenne and parsley together. Store remaining ingredients separately.

In-the-field preparation

Open anchovies and empty into a bowl. Mash with a fork. Add remaining ingredients and stir until smooth. Spread over crackers, bread, bagels, or muffins. Serve.

THIS LUNCH needs no adaptation for car camping, horse, or goat trips, or for backpacking, provided you don't mind the extra weight and serve it over crackers.

Later in the day, when the current picks up a little, we pull out of our lethargy and separate the canoes. The scenery also livens up. Rock formations such as The Sphinx perch high above the water. Turk's Head, a stone variation on a headdress straight out of the movie *Lawrence of Arabia*, and an unnamed pinnacle we dub "Challenger" (because it looks surprisingly like the space shuttle ready for launch) flank the Sphinx. As the canoes glide past this majestic work of nature, I glance back for one last look. But from this direction, Sphinx has transformed itself into Snoopy. That's the funny thing with wind and weather sculptures. Perspective changes them entirely.

Beyond the bend from the Sphinx and its companions, campsites get scarce. Cliffs rise 1,300 feet above the water. Neither Powell nor Dellenbaugh wrote anything about this section of the river. However, George Y. Bradley, who accompanied Powell's first expedition, called this segment of Canyonlands "dark and threatening."

At the entrance to Horse Canyon, we point the canoes at the shore and call it a day. After a short hike up a well-defined animal trail, we discover what must have been an old indigenous campground, littered with flakes and bits of worked jasper. Surrounded by rim rock, our location commands an extensive view of the river as well as back into the canyon.

While the guys haul the sleeping gear up top, Erin helps me set up the kitchen down by the delta of the stream that runs in the bottom of the canyon. Insects swarm everywhere. Bats, too. Ron builds a fire so the smoke will keep the mosquitoes away while we eat. One campfire Powell's men started brought disaster to the expedition.

A whirlwind came up and scattered the fire among some dead willows nearby. The men dashed for the boats, grabbing as much gear as they could carry. "The cook fills his arms with the mess-kit, and jumping into a boat, stumbles and falls, and away go our cooking utensils into the river," stated Powell in the log. "Our plates are gone; our spoons are gone; our knives and forks are gone." To top it off, the bank of willows that hung over the boats caught fire, forcing the men to cut the crafts loose. The swift-flowing water propelled them downstream over a rapid filled with rocks. When the men finally managed to steer the boats ashore again and hiked back to the site of the fire, all they found were "a few tin cups, basins, and a camp kettle; and this is all the mess-kit we now have."

Day Five Dinner Recipes

Turk's Head Ham

2 c. ground ham
1 large onion, diced
2 green chilies, chopped
8 mushrooms, sliced
2 large tomatoes, chopped

1 bell pepper, chopped
1 t. cumin
1 t. parsley flakes
1 T. margarine
1 recipe Wild Side Rice (see Index)

Dehydrate ham, vegetables, mushrooms, and tomatoes. Bag with parsley and cumin. Dry rice according to the recipe.

Cherry Challenger

1 20 oz. can pineapple rings in juice
1 16 oz. can peach halves in juice

1 16 oz. jar maraschino cherries
1/4 c. coconut flakes

Transfer cherries to plastic zipper bag. Bag coconut. Pack cans of fruit.

In-the-field preparation

Hydrate ham mixture while water boils for hot drinks. Place ham mixture and 2 c. cold water in a big pot. Cover. Bring to a boil over high heat. Add margarine. Lower heat and simmer 15 minutes or until food is tender. Add enough water to make 1 1/2 c. of liquid. Return to a boil. Stir in dried rice. Remove from heat. Allow mixture to sit for 10 minutes before serving. Wrap an Ensolite pad around the pot to keep it warm. Reheat a few minutes if it cools too quickly. For dessert, divide pineapple rings among the small bowls, reserving juice. Next divide the cherries, then the peach halves, reserving peach juice. Mix the two juices. Pour over fruit. Sprinkle coconut on top. Serve.

*   **AS AN OPTION** on backpacking trips, dehydrate chopped green chilies and serve dried fruit for dessert. For horse, goat, or car camping trips, this meal needs no adaptation.*

DAY SIX MENU

Breakfast

Fruit Confluence

White Water Biscuits

Coffee

Lunch

Apricots (canned) Mashed with Chopped Walnuts

Smoked Sausages Mashed with Salsa Verde

Juice or Soda

Dinner

Powell Potato Chowder

Green River Vegetable Medley

Jasper Springs Cake

Tea

DAY SIX

July 20. The course of the Green at this point is approximately at right angles to that of the Colorado, and on the brink of the latter canyon we find the same system of terraced and walled glens. The walls and pinnacles and towers are of sandstone, homogeneous in structure but not in color, as they show broad bands of red, buff, and gay.

—John Wesley Powell

Not all of Powell's food entries involved hardship. When a string of bad luck looked like it might end the expedition, the 1869 group stumbled upon a man and his two sons scouting a location for a town on the river bank. They sent a messenger to a town twenty miles up the valley. The next day, a wagon arrived with a cornucopia of supplies and a rare treat: "two or three dozen melons."

Day Six Breakfast Recipes

Fruit Confluence

1 honeydew melon	**3/4** c. chopped dates
1 20 oz. can crushed pineapple in juice	**3/4** c. chopped walnuts
4 oranges	**3** 6 oz. containers custard style
4 bananas	strawberry yogurt

Bag dates and nuts together. Pack remaining ingredients. (Choose an underripe melon so it will ripen during the trip and be just right on day six.) Store yogurt in the ice chest.

White Water Biscuits

2 c. flour	**1** t. baking powder
4 T. powdered buttermilk	**1** t. baking soda
1 t. salt	**3** T. margarine

Blend and bag all ingredients except margarine.

In-the-field preparation

Cut margarine into biscuit mix. Add 1 1/4 c. of cold water to dry ingredients or enough to form a soft dough. Pat into biscuits about 1/2 inch thick. Bake in the skillet with a lid fire 10–15 minutes until lightly browned. Makes 12–14. Open the pineapple, draining liquid (reserve it to add to tea for a different flavor). Peel and chop melon, oranges, and bananas. In the large pot, mix all ingredients. Stir well and serve.

THIS MEAL is only suitable as a first-day horse or goat trip breakfast. No adaptation is needed for car camping.

From Horse Canyon, it's an easy float to the confluence of the Green and Colorado rivers. So we take a long lunch break at Jasper Canyon, exploring it. Brush grows thick at the mouth of the draw, forcing us to bushwhack our way through. Jasper Springs Creek meanders through the canyon floor. We follow it. Fossilized crab and worm tracks decorate limestone chunks that litter the bank. Then the creek opens into an amphitheater of rim rock. Water spills over the edge, falling into a pool three hundred feet below. An irresistible spot for an afternoon dip, we strip down to our swim suits and wade in. Sun warmed, the clear water creates a luxurious, refreshing sensation. An hour passes then two. None of us wish to leave, but we want to make the confluence before dark. So we retrace our steps and climb back into the boats.

The White Rim of Stillwater Canyon turns into a series of grotesque rock formations as we float nearer to the confluence. Cliffs a thousand feet high tower above us, binding us within the narrow confines of the river. Stone outcroppings that resemble surreal-shaped birds with serrated beaks and gouged eyes stare down on us. When the walls give way to the Y of the confluence and a wide sandbar just around the bend on the Colorado, I feel a sense of anticlimax. Two grand rivers come together after flowing through incredible walls of rock. They comingle more mud and silt than water and gurgle along as if the separate rivers never existed. As we beach the canoes, I notice fresh deer prints in the wet sand.

The 1869 party stopped to hunt whenever they spotted game in an area where they could bring the boats ashore. One hunt resulted in a feast. "And a feast it is!" Powell exclaimed in his log. "Two fine young [mountain] sheep! We care not for bread or beans or dried apples to-night; coffee and mutton are all we ask." Our last-night-on-the-river feast differs from Powell's, but we enjoy it with the same excitement he expressed.

Day Six Dinner Recipes

Powell Potato Chowder

1 10 oz. can baby clams in water

5 potatoes

1 onion

10 mushrooms, sliced thin

1 T. parsley flakes

1/2 t. thyme

1 t. pepper

1/2 c. powdered milk

1 t. salt

2 T. margarine

Dehydrate mushrooms. Bag them together with parsley, thyme, pepper, milk, and salt. Store onion and potatoes in net bags. Pack canned clams. Store margarine separately.

Green River Vegetable Medley

2 yellow squash, sliced

20 okra, chopped

1 cucumber, sliced

12 mushrooms, sliced

2 t. thyme

2 T. soy sauce

2 T. margarine

Dehydrate vegetables and bag together with the thyme. Store soy sauce in a small plastic bottle. Keep margarine separate.

Jasper Springs Cake

2 c. flour

2 T. sugar

1 t. baking powder

1 t. ground cloves

1 t. mace

1 t. cinnamon

1 c. raisins

l/2 c. honey

1 egg

1/4 c. plus 1 T. margarine

Mix and bag all ingredients except raisins, honey, egg, and margarine. Bag raisins separately. Place honey in a plastic bottle . Store margarine and egg in the ice chest.

In-the-field preparation

Rehydrate Green River Vegetable Medley and mushroom mixture for the chowder. Remove egg and margarine from the ice chest to warm up to outside temperature. Slice potatoes thin and chop onion. Fill pot half full of water and pour in clams and juice. Add potatoes, onion, mushroom mixture, and 2 T. margarine. Cover and bring to a boil over high heat. Reduce heat to low and continue to cook until potatoes are done, stirring occasionally. Meanwhile, pour vegetables into the skillet. Add soy sauce, 2 T. margarine, and enough water to cover the bottom of the skillet. Cover. Steam until vegetables are tender, 10–15 minutes. Add more water as needed. Serve. For dessert, melt 1 T. margarine in skillet and set aside. Beat l/4 c. margarine and sugar together in large pot. Add egg then honey then 1/2 c. water, beating well each time. Stir in flour mixture, When completely moistened, pour into skillet. Bake over low heat with a lid fire for 40–50 minutes.

THIS MEAL needs no adaptation for car camping, horse, or goat trips. For backpacking, dehydrate clams.

DAY SEVEN MENU

Breakfast

Last Day Lyonnais

Tea

Lunch

Peanut Butter with Chopped Dates

Raisins Chopped with Orange Sections

Juice or Soda

Dinner

Dellenbaugh's Anvil

Ricochet Bats

Tea

DAY SEVEN

July 18. The day is spent in obtaining the time and spreading our rations, which we find are badly injured. The flour has been wet and dried so many times that it is all musty and full of hard lumps. We make a sieve of mosquito netting and run our flour through it, losing more than 200 pounds by the process.

—John Wesley Powell

Satisfaction and sadness stir in camp this morning. Unlike Powell's expedition, which continued until November 1, 1869, today our journey ends with a sixty-mile jet boat trip up the Colorado to Moab. We scatter in different directions at sunrise to say personal good-byes to the river. Breakfast is, as Powell wrote on day three of his men's mutiny (unable to stand the treacherous rapids and lack of food any longer) "as solemn as a funeral."

Day Seven Breakfast Recipe

Last Day Lyonnais

4 eggs
1 small onion
1 clove garlic
3 T. margarine

1 T. flour
2 T. parsley flakes
1/4 c. powdered milk
4 bagels

Bag milk and parsley. Put onion and garlic in a net bag. Store remaining ingredients separately.

In-the-field preparation

Put eggs in large pot of water. Cover and bring to a boil over high heat, warming bagels on top of the lid (or in the skillet over low heat with a two-burner stove). Boil 10 minutes and remove from heat. Meanwhile, chop onion and garlic. Melt margarine in the skillet. Add 1 c. water to milk and mix. Set aside. Sauté onion and garlic in margarine for 1 minute over high heat, stirring constantly. Add flour. Stir until absorbed. Add milk. Stir and heat over medium heat until gravy bubbles and thickens. Cover and set aside. Peel eggs, reserving water for tea. Chop eggs and add to gravy. Serve over bagels.

THIS MEAL needs no adaptation for horse, car camping, or goat trips. (However, since bagels will turn moldy after a few days without refrigeration, serve early in the trip.) For backpacking, take only if you don't mind the extra weight.

I had stocked a full set of meals for the seventh day even though we'd arranged for the jet boat to meet us this morning. Afternoon arrives. The boat doesn't. Engine problems delay it until late in the day. The extra food means we don't need to ration supplies like Powell did in this same spot "for it became evident that we would run short of food before we could get any more," he noted.

Day Seven Dinner Recipes

Dellenbaugh's Anvil

1/2 lb. turkey sausage
1 eggplant, chopped
2 large tomatoes, chopped
1/2 bell pepper, chopped

1 onion, chopped
1 T. black pepper
2 T. margarine
3 c. egg noodles

Brown sausage. Dry meat, eggplant, tomatoes, bell pepper, and onion. Bag meat and onion together. Bag vegetables, tomatoes, and black pepper. Bag egg noodles separately.

Ricochet Bars

1 c. flour
1 t. baking powder
1 t. salt
1 T. Amaretto-flavored coffee drink
1/2 c. nuts, chopped

1/2 c. miniature marshmallows
1/2 c. semisweet chocolate chips
1/3 c. molasses
1 egg
5 T. margarine

Mix and bag flour, baking powder, and salt. Mix and bag together nuts, marshmallows, and chocolate chips. Pack a plastic container of molasses. Store egg and margarine separately.

In-the-field preparation

Fill a pot with cold water. Cover and bring to a boil over high heat. Reconstitute meat and vegetables in bags on the lid while water comes to a boil. Remove pot from stove. Make hot drinks with half the water. Insulate the remaining water by wrapping an Ensolite pad around the pot to keep it warm. Melt 2 T. margarine in the skillet over high heat. Add meat. Cover and cook until tender, adding water as it becomes absorbed. Add vegetables and a cup of cold water. Bring to a boil, adding enough water to maintain about a cup of liquid in the bottom of the skillet. Boil for two minutes. Remove from heat and keep warm.

Return the pot of water to the stove. Over high heat, bring to boil again. Add egg noodles and cook until tender. Serve sausage/vegetable mixture over drained noodles. For dessert, melt margarine in the skillet. In a pot combine 5 T. margarine, molasses, and egg. Stir in flour mixture and spread in the skillet. Top with marshmallows, chocolate chips, and nut mixture. Bake over low heat with a lid fire for 15–20 minutes. Cut and serve.

THIS MEAL *needs no adaptation for backpacking, car camping, horse, or goat trips.*

WANT MORE HISTORY?

A Country Kitchen, 1850. Maynard, MA: Chandler Press, 1987.

Back, Joe. *Horses, Hitches & Rocky Trails: "The Packers Bible."* Boulder, CO: Johnson Books, 1987.

Blair, Bob, ed. *William Henry Jackson's "The Pioneer Photographer."* Santa Fe, NM: Museum of New Mexico Press, 2005.

Butruille, Susan G. *Women's Voices from the Oregon Trail.* Boise, ID: Tamarack Books. 1993.

Child, Lydia M. *The American Frugal Housewife.* Bedford, MA: Applewood Books, 1832.

Coyle, L. Patrick Jr. *The World Encyclopedia of Food.* New York: Facts On File, 1982.

Delano, A. *Life on the Plains and at the Diggings.* Buffalo, NY: Miller, Orton & Mulligan, 1854.

Dellenbaugh, Frederick S. *The Romance of the Colorado River: The Story of its Discovery in 1540, with an Account of the Later Explorations, and with Special Reference to the Voyages of Powell through the Line of the Great Canyons.* New York: G.P. Putnam's Sons, 1902.

Grinnell, George B. *The Cheyenne Indians: Their History and Ways of Life.* Vols. 1 and 2. Lincoln, NE: University of Nebraska Press, 1923.

Hamilton, William T. *My Sixty Years on the Plains.* New York: Knickerbocker Press, 1905.

Hartwell, Marcia B. *A Sampler of Recipes 1796 to 1908.* Northampton, MA: Hartwell, 1984.

Kalman, Bobbie. *Food for the Settler.* New York: Crabtree Publishing Co., 1982.

Lee, Hilde G. *Taste of the States: A Food History of America.* Charlottesville, VA: Howell Press, 1992.

Marcy, Randolph B. *The Prairie Traveler.* Old Saybrook, CT: Applewood Books, 1859.

McPhee, John. *Rising from the Plains.* New York: Farrar, Straus, Giroux, 1986.

Merrill, Marlene Deahl, ed. *Seeing Yellowstone in 1871: Earliest Descriptions and Images from the Field.* Lincoln, NE: University of Nebraska Press, 2005.

Miller, Alfred J. *The West of Alfred Jacob Miller.* Ed. Marvin C. Ross. Norman, OK: University of Oklahoma Press, 1968.

Powell, John W. *The Exploration of the Colorado River and Its Canyons.* New York: Dover Publications, reprinted 1961.

Reedstrom, Ernest L. *Historic Dress of the Old West*. New York: Blandford Press. 1986.

Rickey, Don. *Forty Miles A Day On Beans and Hay*. Norman, OK: University of Oklahoma Press, 1963.

Riggs, Stephen R. *Mary and I: Forty Years with the Sioux*. Williamstown, MA: Corner House Publishers, reprinted 1971.

Roast, Waverly and Richard de Rochemont. *Eating in America: A History*. New York: William Morrow & Co., 1976.

Stewart, Elinore Pruitt. *Letters of a Woman Homesteader*. Lincoln, NE: University of Nebraska Press, 1961.

Trenholm, Virginia C., and Maurine Carley. *The Shoshonis: Sentinels of the Rockies*. Norman, OK: University of Oklahoma Press, 1964.

Walker, Mrs. Elkanah and Mrs. Cushing Eells. *First White Women Over the Rockies: Diaries, Letters, and Biographical Sketches of the Six Women of the Oregon Mission who made the Overland Journey in 1836 and 1838*. Vols. 1-3. Glendale, CA: Arthur H. Clark Co., 1963.

Webber, Bert, ed. *Diary of lane Gould in 1862*. Medford, OR: Webb Research Group, Publishers, 1993.

Williams, Mary L., ed. *An Army Wife's Cookbook With Household Hints and Home Remedies*. Tucson, AZ: Southwest Parks and Monuments Association, 1972.

Zwinger, Ann. Run River, Run: *A Naturalist's Journey Down One of the Great Rivers of the West*. New York: Harper & Row. Publishers, 1975.

INDEX